Achieving **QTLS**

The Minimum Core for
Information and Communication Technology
Audit and Test

Achieving **QTLS**

The Minimum Core for
Information and Communication Technology
Audit and Test

Sandra Murray

LearningMatters

First published in 2009 by Learning Matters Ltd

British Library Cataloguing in Publication Data
A CIP record for this book is available from the British Library.

ISBN: 978 1 84445 288 0

Cover design by Topics – The Creative Partnership
Text design by Code 5
Project management by Deer Park Productions, Tavistock, Devon
Typeset by PDQ Typesetting Ltd, Newcastle under Lyme
Printed and bound in Great Britain by Bell & Bain Ltd, Glasgow

Learning Matters Ltd
33 Southernhay East
Exeter EX1 1NX
Tel: 01392 215560
info@learningmatters.co.uk
www.learningmatters.co.uk

Contents

The author

Sandra Murray is an Advanced Practitioner and Lecturer in Teacher Training at Newcastle under Lyme College, teaching on PTLLS and DTLLS courses. Prior to working in ITT, Sandra taught ICT and was an ILT champion, supporting teachers incorporating ICT into their teaching.

Acknowledgements

For Grace and James and for Mary, who set me on this path.

Microsoft product screenshots reprinted with permission from Microsoft Corporation.

Every effort has been made to trace the copyright holders and to obtain their permission for the use of copyright material. The publisher and author will gladly receive any information enabling them to rectify any error or omission in subsequent editions.

1
Why do trainee teachers need to meet the minimum core requirements?

Reform of teacher training

The reform of initial teacher training in the lifelong learning sector resulted in the introduction of a range of sector specific teaching qualifications with effect from September 2007. The reforms require that those with a full teaching role achieve Qualified Teacher Learning and Skills status (QTLS). For those with significantly less than a full teaching role, for example, trainers delivering material prepared by others, the requirement is to achieve Associate Teacher Learning and Skills (ATLS) status.

To achieve QTLS teachers need to complete the Diploma in Teaching in the Lifelong Learning Sector (DTLLS), whereas to achieve ATLS, teachers need to complete the Certificate in Teaching in the Lifelong Learning Sector (CTLLS). QTLS or ATLS is awarded following successful completion of professional formation.

Whereas teachers in other areas of the lifelong learning sector can be seen to have either an associate or full teaching role, Skills for Life lecturers are automatically assumed to have a full teaching role. Because of this they are required to follow a specialised Skills for Life route to QTLS.

The new qualifications followed a series of consultations in which it was recognised that in addition to developing teaching skills, teachers and trainers in the learning and skills sector also required skills in literacy, language, numeracy and information and communication technology (ICT) in order to function effectively and support their learners. These skills are met by the introduction of the minimum core, an integral part of the qualifications.

What is the minimum core?

The minimum core identifies the minimum skills and knowledge required by teachers in the lifelong learning sector in three key areas: literacy and language, numeracy and ICT.

The minimum core in ICT comprises:

Part A: Knowledge and Understanding

A1 Personal and social factors influencing ICT learning and development
A2 Explicit knowledge about ICT

Part B: Personal ICT skills

Communications
Processes

Those teachers in a full teaching role are required to meet both Part A – Knowledge and Understanding and Part B – Personal ICT skills, whereas those in an associate role need to meet Part B – Personal ICT skills.

This book will cover the entire minimum core for ICT relevant to both QTLS and ATLS and will develop, audit and test your knowledge, understanding and personal ICT skills, for use within and outside of the classroom.

REFERENCES AND FURTHER READING REFERENCES AND FURTHER READING

DfES (2004) *Equipping our teachers for the future: reforming initial teacher training for the learning and skills sector.* Nottingham: DfES Publications

DfES (2007) *Initial teacher training – making the reforms happen, learning and skills sector.* Nottingham: DfES Publications

LLUK (2007) *Addressing literacy, language, numeracy and ICT needs in education and training: Defining the minimum core of teachers' knowledge, understanding and personal skills. A guide for initial teacher education programmes.* London: LLUK

2
Skills audit

This skills audit will enable you to consider your skills and knowledge in relation to the key areas of the minimum core in ICT. You should consider each area and grade yourself according to what you consider your level of knowledge and skills to be in each area. Grade yourself on a scale of 1 to 5, with 1 being less able and 5 being most able.

Personal, social and cultural factors influencing ICT learning and development	1	2	3	4	5
Be aware of the different factors affecting the acquisition and development of ICT skills					
Be aware of the importance of ICT in enabling users to participate in and gain access to society and the modern economy					
Understand the range of learners' technological and educational backgrounds					
Identify the main learning disabilities and difficulties relating to ICT learning and skill development					
Identify the potential barriers that inhibit ICT skills development					
Explicit knowledge about ICT	1	2	3	4	5
Make and use decisions about understanding					
Communicating processes and understandings					
Demonstrate purposeful use of ICT					
Identify essential characteristics of ICT					
Identify how learners develop ICT skills					
Personal ICT skills	1	2	3	4	5
Communicate with others with/about ICT in an open and supportive manner					
Assess own and other people's understanding					
Express yourself clearly and accurately					
Communicate about/with ICT in a variety of ways that suit and support the intended audience and recognise such use by others					
Use appropriate techniques to reinforce oral communication, check how well the information is received and support understanding of those listening					
Use ICT systems					
Find, select and exchange information					
Develop and present information					

Source: *Addressing literacy, language, numeracy and ICT needs in education and training: Defining the minimum core of teachers' knowledge, understanding and personal skills. A guide for initial teacher education programmes.* LLUK, 2007 pp 40–55.

3
Communicating ICT

By the end of this chapter you should be able to:

- **identify methods and purposes of assessment in ICT;**
- **identify common computer terminology;**
- **suggest effective ways to communicate ICT depending on audience;**
- **communicate with others about ICT.**

This chapter relates to the following minimum core requirements:

A2 Making and using decisions about understanding.

Communicating processes and understanding.

B Communicate with others about ICT in an open and supportive manner.

Assess own, and other people's, understanding.

Express yourself clearly and accurately.

Communicate about/with ICT in a variety of ways that suit and support the intended audience, and recognise such use by others.

Use appropriate techniques to reinforce oral communication, check how well the information is received and support understanding of those listening.

This chapter also contributes to the following LLUK Standards:

BK3.4, BP3.4, BK4.1, BP4.1, CK3.2, CP3.2, CP4.2, EK1.1, EP1.1, EK1.2, EP1.2, EK1.3, EP1.3 EK2.1, EP2.1, EP2.3, EP3.1.

Within any teaching area, the need for clear and effective two-way communication is paramount. When considering ICT, this is no less essential, therefore this chapter will examine communication in ICT, both for teaching and assessment, noting the nature of ICT language in terms of specialist terminology.

Key information

Methods and purposes of assessment in ICT

Assessment can be undertaken for a range of reasons and allows the teacher to find out what learners know. This is essential in the effective planning of your course, to enable you to teach effectively, to differentiate and to provide an inclusive environment for your learners. Initial, diagnostic, formative and summative assessment all have their role to play.

Initial assessment

ICT as a subject area has its own terminology which needs to be considered carefully to ensure that it does not become a barrier to learning. A teacher of ICT would not walk into a classroom and launch into a jargon-laden lecture with a group of learners without finding out what they already knew about the subject and what terminology they were aware of. Initial assessment, therefore, is essential.

Initial assessment takes place prior to or at the start of a course and can be undertaken in a number of ways, the appropriateness of which should be considered in relation to the group of learners.

One method of initial assessment is self assessment, whereby learners examine what they know (or think they know) and match it to specified criteria, for example, as is the case with the skills audit in this book. This has the advantage that learners can complete the self assessment in their own time. However, a disadvantage of this method of assessment is that bias may be introduced. This bias may be dependent on learner confidence or interpretation of the criteria, some may overstate and some understate their abilities in certain areas. Other methods of initial assessment could be interview, test or practical activity.

EXAMPLE

When assessing ICT it is important not just to assess practical skills. Underpinning knowledge is just as important. For example, a learner may be able to copy formulas into a spreadsheet, but may not know how the formula is constructed.

An initial assessment can also be utilised for other reasons. In order to effectively account for a variation in learning styles, a learning styles analysis can be undertaken to ascertain whether your learners have visual, auditory or kinaesthetic characteristics.

Spiky profiles

ICT is one area of learning that is particularly broad, encompassing a wide range of areas. A learner may be particularly confident in using a computer to watch movies and download music, but have only limited experience in using office software. When a learner has a range of skills – some strong, some weak – they are said to have a spiky profile. An initial or diagnostic assessment should help to identify learners' overall skills and knowledge in this area.

Diagnostic assessment

Should a more detailed assessment be required, this is the role of diagnostic assessment. Diagnostic assessment gives a more in-depth result of strengths and areas for development and can form a strong basis for an individual learning plan.

Formative assessment

Ongoing assessment of ICT skills, as with any area, is necessary to ensure that learning is taking place. This is the role of formative assessment, also known as assessment for learning when linked to identifying how to improve learning, Black and Wiliam (1998).

Observation combined with corrected practice is one way of assessing and developing practical skills. Talking to the learners can be an excellent way of undertaking formative assessment and will allow you to see how they are progressing. Other methods could include test or practical activity. Formative assessment of knowledge can be undertaken in a number of ways, which include question and answer (Q&A) at the appropriate level, quiz, gapped handout or written test.

Summative assessment

Summative assessment of ICT skills identifies the knowledge or skills that the learners have gained by the end of the course. This can take many forms, which may include the creation of a portfolio of evidence, a written test or exam, or project.

An important note regarding assessment is the ongoing assessment of your own knowledge and skills. For a teacher, an essential skill is the ability to self assess and reflect on own knowledge and experience, which can form the basis of future development. These skills will become an integral part of your course.

Effective communication of ICT

The language of ICT can be a little daunting, with a range of acronyms and specialist terminology. Awareness of this is important to you as a teacher in order to ensure effective communication with your learners. Initial assessment can assist in identifying what terminology learners may be familiar with, though it is important not to make assumptions and to explain acronyms on their first use.

HINTS AND TIPS

An effective way of introducing terminology to your learners is to give them a sheet containing the terminology you will be using alongside definitions. As your learners develop in confidence you could revise the sheet to a gapped handout in order that the learners can identify the definitions themselves.

EXAMPLE
Common computer terminology

Terminology	Definition	Example
Software	Programs used by the computer	Office software, games
Operating system	Controls software and hardware	Windows, Linux
Hardware	Physical components of computer	Processor, Monitor
RAM	Random Access Memory	2GB RAM
CPU	Central Processing Unit	Intel 1.6GHZ Processor
Peripherals	Additional, external hardware	Printer
Hard drive	Computer's main storage	160GB Hard drive

It is only natural that some learners may misunderstand and use incorrect terminology at times. When this occurs, the learners should be corrected and the reason for the misunderstanding identified. It is crucial that this is provided in a supportive manner in order not to create barriers and ensure firm foundations for future learning.

Enhancing communication

Communicating concepts related to ICT can be enhanced with the use of images and examples relevant to the learners. Careful consideration should be given as to how communication occurs, verbally, non-verbally and also via use of resources such as handouts – the size of text, use of images and language all play an important part.

Two-way communication is of course, essential. It is not enough for a teacher to be able to deliver information, they need to listen to learners and interpret body language and other non-verbal communication. Often, when a learner does not understand they do not say anything for fear of being set apart from the rest of the class. The ability to interpret non-verbal communication can assist in supporting learners in this, or similar circumstances.

Communication of ICT can be further enhanced via use of metaphor and analogy. A metaphor is used when we say that one thing is another, for example when we refer to the CPU as being the 'brains' of the computer. Analogy, whereby a new term is linked to something familiar to the learner, is particularly effective in communicating ICT.

Different teaching and communication methods will be necessary depending on the learning situation and also the size of the group. For a large group you may find the use of a projector with video clips and images useful. However, for a small group and individual learners, a handout or single computer may be more appropriate.

Whilst communicating with learners effectively is essential, the ability to communicate with colleagues is equally so. By working with colleagues you can discuss what went well, what did not go so well and by sharing best practices and experiences, further development of ICT skills will occur.

Effective communication with ICT

ICT comprises a range of communication tools including e-mail, learning environments and mobile communication devices. By communicating with learners using these tools you will be developing both your own and their skills. Consider the example whereby you want to develop your learners' e-mail skills. What better way to do this than to use e-mail as a method of communication.

Key questions

Q1   What is hardware?

    a) A peripheral
    b) A way of accessing a computer
    c) Physical components of the computer
    d) A device connected to a PC via a cable

Q2   What is software?

    a) Programs used by the computer
    b) A floppy disk
    c) Devices connected to a PC via a cable
    d) A peripheral

Q3   Which of the following are hardware? (Select all that apply.)

    a) Operating system
    b) Mouse
    c) Keyboard
    d) Speakers

Q4   What is Windows?

a) A specific type of high resolution monitor
b) A type of hardware
c) An operating system
d) A peripheral

Q5   Which of the following is the 'brains' of the computer?

a) RAM
b) CPU
c) Hard drive
d) Operating system

Q6   What is RAM?

a) Temporary memory
b) Long-term memory
c) A type of processor
d) Part of the hard drive

Q7   What is a spiky profile?

a) Identification of learners reluctant to use ICT
b) Identification of learners keen to use ICT
c) A mix of skill levels
d) Consistent skill levels

Q8   Should you comment when learners misunderstand terminology?

a) Yes, you can assume that they won't mind.
b) No, you can assume that their peer group will correct them.
c) No, this might alienate the learners.
d) Yes, but don't make an issue, and be supportive.

Q9   Which of the following would be most appropriate to enhance communication in a one-to-one teaching session?

a) A laptop and projector
b) A laptop
c) A large print handout

Q10 Self assessment is important because (select all that apply):

a) It saves the teacher work.
b) Learners learn more effectively by identifying own areas for development.
c) It is required by observers.
d) It encourages reflection.

Q11 The following are common terminology referring to use of a PC and the internet. Match the terminology with its definition.

1. Internet	A. Interconnected pages accessed via the internet
2. World wide web	B. Used to search for information over the web
3. URL	C. Web browser
4. Internet Explorer	D. Windows file management system
5. Windows Explorer	E. Global network of computers
6. Search engine	F. Address of a web page

Q12 This question will ask you to consider how to enhance communication in different situations.

a) You have created a set of typed instructions which tell learners how to use a search engine as part of an independent task. The instructions are in size 14 font and comprise five paragraphs. In the past, learners have had problems following the instructions. What can you do to enhance communication in this situation?

b) You have inherited a PowerPoint presentation that provides detailed background to the history of the National Health Service. The presentation is very informative and contains a large amount of text in size 16 font. You know that this information will be very useful to your learners, but need to make revisions to enhance communication. What do you suggest?

c) You have been asked to deliver a lecture to a group of 60 learners. You have been provided with a course handout which is 12 pages long, but does contain images and is well presented. Learners have expressed dissatisfaction with this session as previously the learners were given the handout and asked to read it through. What suggestions can you give to enhance communication in this session?

d) As part of your course you are required to observe a colleague and comment on their practice. They are teaching a group of learners with learning disabilities about shapes, but do this by describing the shape. Can you suggest how to enhance communication?

Q13 Identify whether the following are true or false.

a) Formative assessment only takes place at the end of the session.   True/False
b) Initial assessment is the same as diagnostic assessment.   True/False
c) Question and answer is one method of formative assessment.   True/False
d) Summative assessment takes place at the end of a course.   True/False
e) Peer assessment is undertaken by the teacher.   True/False
f) Self assessment is mainly ineffective.   True/False
g) Diagnostic assessment often takes place at the end of the course.   True/False
h) Assessment for learning always takes place at the start of the course.   True/False
i) Examination is one method of summative assessment.   True/False
j) Diagnostic assessment is more detailed than initial assessment.   True/False

Q14 This question requires that you consider the appropriateness of different assessment methods to assess ICT skills.

a) You plan to use observation to assess the ICT skills of a group of learners whilst they perform a workbook-based task. What are the advantages and disadvantages of this?

b) You have decided that one-to-one interviews will be an effective way to ascertain learners' prior skills in using ICT. What are the advantages and disadvantages of this?

c) You have set an ICT-based homework task as a method of formatively assessing learners' ICT skills. What are the advantages and disadvantages of this?

Q15 Consider the extracts below, which are excerpts of instructions to learners. These instructions have worked well for previous groups who were confident computer users. However, the new cohort will be a group of learners who have not used a computer before. For this activity you are asked to suggest why the terminology used may be a barrier to communication.

a) 'Log on to the computers using the user name and password.'
b) 'Change the font size to 12.'
c) 'Use the calculator on the computer to add together the list of numbers on your handout.'
d) 'Shut down your computer.'
e) 'Open Microsoft Word using the shortcut on the desktop.'

A SUMMARY OF KEY POINTS

In this chapter we have looked at the following key points.

> **Communication lies at the core of ICT and has been considered in terms of communication with, and of, technology.**

> **The nature of ICT-specific terminology.**

> **Ways of preventing barriers to learning due to communication in relation to a range of types and methods of assessment.**

REFERENCES AND FURTHER READING REFERENCES AND FURTHER READING

Black, P and Wiliam, D (1998) *Inside the black box: raising standards through classroom assessment*. London: Kings College London
Tummons, J (2007) *Assessing learning in the lifelong learning sector*. Exeter: Learning Matters

Websites

Assessment for ICT learners: http://excellence.qia.org.uk/page.aspx?o=127906

4
Personal, social and cultural factors influencing ICT learning and development

By the end of this chapter you should be able to:

- **identify personal and social factors influencing ICT learning and development;**
- **suggest ways of overcoming potential barriers to ICT use;**
- **identify legislation relevant to ICT use;**
- **suggest how the use of ICT can contribute to an inclusive learning environment.**

This chapter relates to the following minimum core requirements:

A1 The different factors affecting the acquisition and development of ICT skills.

The importance of ICT in enabling users to participate in public life, society and the modern economy.

The range of learners' technological and educational backgrounds.

The main learning disabilities and difficulties relating to ICT learning and development.

Potential barriers that inhibit ICT development.

How learners develop ICT skills.

This chapter also contributes to the following LLUK Standards:
BK5.2, BP5.2, DK1.1, DP1.1.

As you progress through your DTLLS course you will consider personal, social and cultural factors influencing learning. This chapter will consider these areas relevant to the minimum core area of ICT and will involve identification and removal of potential barriers to learning and creation of an inclusive learning environment.

Key information

Attitudes in society

The development of learners' and tutors' ICT skills and their implementation within the classroom requires consideration of learner attitudes to ICT use. These attitudes may involve legal, moral and security considerations of which the tutor needs to be aware.

Social attitudes to file sharing and illegal copying and downloading

Many educational organisations have policies governing acceptable use of ICT. As a tutor using ICT in lessons, it is essential that you are aware of relevant legislation. If your learners have access to the internet, you need to ensure that you know what is and isn't legal in terms of ICT use.

One growing area of technology is file sharing – whereby music files can be shared amongst large communities, often illegally and contrary to the Copyright, Designs and Patents Act, 1988. More recently, due to court action, many of the file sharing websites have been closed down and are being replaced by legal versions. If your learners are going to be using the internet, you need ensure that your learners are aware of the relevant legislation and implications of illegal file sharing.

In addition to file sharing, learners may think that it is acceptable to copy software or download files from unauthorised websites. It is part of a teacher's role to ensure that learners are informed in this area.

Viruses, spam and phishing

The security of the internet is another key issue and users may feel threatened by viruses and phishing (see Hints and Tips below). The creation and distribution of these is illegal under the 1990 Computer Misuse act. Viruses, are computer programs created with malicious intent and they can cause irreparable damage to computer software. They are distributed in a number of ways including sharing of files and opening unknown e-mail attachments, which may contain a virus.

HINTS AND TIPS

The use of e-mail has caused a variation on traditional paper-based junk mail – in this case, spam. Spam is unsolicited e-mail, and can be genuine, random marketing or created with fraudulent intentions. The best practice is to delete unsolicited e-mails without opening them.

Phishing is one of the latest developments on the internet and involves users being directed to genuine-looking websites (often via a plausible e-mail link) with the intent of gaining bank details, passwords and enabling subsequent fraudulent activity.

Unsuitable materials

It is quite possible that navigation of the web may lead to unsuitable websites. Search engine results may include links that lead to inappropriate sites or images via an image search. Whilst organisational settings may prevent access to unsuitable websites and help to protect the user it is unlikely that they would prevent all unsuitable material, therefore it is clear that caution and supervision of learners is necessary when performing web searches.

Age

Learners in the lifelong learning sector can vary in age from 14 and beyond, often including mature learners who may not have had any formal ICT training. ICT is widely taught in schools, though that does not mean that all school leavers will necessarily be competent in this area. Barriers including learning difficulties, low confidence and absences from school may lead to poor ICT skills in this age group.

Some older learners including senior citizens may have their own barriers in terms of self efficacy and their belief in their ability to use ICT due to lack of any formal training. However, it is important not to make assumptions as to ability for any group of learners, whatever their age.

Motivational factors

Learner motivation is a key factor influencing success or otherwise, with the area of ICT being no different to any other. The growing use of ICT both in the home and at work can be a key motivator, with learners using e-mail and chat facilities to keep in contact with family and friends worldwide. In terms of the workplace, the growth of ICT means that securing a job and career development can often rely heavily on the ability to use a range of technologies.

ICT can be an effective tool used to develop skills in a number of key skills areas, for example, literacy, language and numeracy. Learners with prior barriers in these areas often find that the use of ICT enhances their learning.

EXAMPLE

A current innovation within education is the incorporation or embedding of these key skills into ICT courses. Numeracy could be embedded into the teaching of spread-sheets by getting learners to manually predict the outcome of formulas and functions. Literacy could be embedded into word processing by getting learners to revise text into paragraphs or add punctuation to text.

Gender

Consideration needs to be given to gender, to avoid stereotyping from the teachers' view-point, and also in terms of how gender may affect the development of ICT skills. Some female learners may give up work to raise a family and as a result may be excluded from ICT developments that their male working counterparts experience on a daily basis.

Therefore, it is important that all learners, irrespective of gender, have their backgrounds taken into consideration in order that an inclusive learning environment may be provided and give equal opportunity for success.

Socio-economic factors

The assumption of access to ICT is one area that needs to be challenged. Learners from low income families may not have the same access to technology as their more affluent counter-parts (known as the digital divide). It is important to make efforts to offer all learners the same opportunity, perhaps by suggesting alternative computer access at a local library or learning resource centre within the organisation.

The development of broadband as the predominant means of accessing the internet could prove to be another issue in preventing equality and inclusion of learners. Not all areas of the country have access to this technology and this should be considered, as should be the costs to keep up to date with these technologies. The ongoing and potentially limitless development in this area means that a one-off investment in ICT equipment may not be enough, neither in time, knowledge nor financial cost.

Ethnicity

The growth of the United Kingdom as a multicultural society requires that diversity is considered in the use of ICT. Learners from other countries may have had limited access to ICT and may require additional support and consideration in the learning environment. For learners who have English as a second or subsequent language, you need to be aware of the terminology that you use that may not translate easily. Phrases such as 'phishing', would doubtless be poorly translated in a wide range of languages.

Disabilities and specific learning difficulties

Disabilities

Learners with disabilities or learning difficulties should not be prevented from gaining access to ICT. As with all areas of education, learners with disabilities are considered as part of the Special Educational Needs and Disability Act, or SENDA (2001) – a revision to the Disability Discrimination Act to include education.

SENDA requires that reasonable adjustments are made to ensure that learners are not placed at a substantial disadvantage to non-disabled learners.

Learners can be further included via use of assistive technologies. This includes software and hardware ranging from keyboard and mouse variations, speech recognition and recording devices, and magnification software for visually impaired learners.

> **EXAMPLE**
>
> Options for supporting a learner with a visual impairment may include large text handouts, a larger screen and keyboard and magnification software.

Specific learning difficulties

Whilst teachers are not expected to be an expert in all specific learning difficulties, they need to show awareness in order that they may support learners within their teaching role.

The most widely known specific learning difficulty is dyslexia. The characteristics of dyslexia are recognised by the British Dyslexia Association (2009) as:

> *Difficulties with phonological processing, rapid naming, working memory, processing speed, and the automatic development of skills that may not match up to an individual's other cognitive abilities.*

Some learners with dyslexia find that the use of coloured paper or a different coloured background can assist with reading, though this is not always the case. You should speak to learners to ascertain if they have any individual requirements which can be provided in class or with additional support.

Key questions

Q1   What is SPAM?

    a) A type of computer virus
    b) Unsolicited e-mail
    c) Society for Protection of Automated Mail
    d) Illegal copying of software

Q2   What is phishing?

    a) Use of e-mail containing a virus
    b) Sending of bulk e-mail
    c) An attempt to obtain passwords and account details via fraudulent e-mail
    d) Creation of a virus

Q3   What is a virus?

a) A way of preventing unsolicited e-mail
b) Unsolicited e-mail
c) A way of deleting unwanted files from a computer
d) A computer program designed with malicious intent

Q4   What is the digital divide?

a) A method of providing internet services
b) The way that a telephone line provides a digital service
c) The gap between those who have access to digital technology and those who do not
d) A more efficient way of accessing digital technology

Q5   What is the purpose of a firewall?

a) To help to protect a computer from external attacks
b) To protect the hard drive of a computer in the event of a fire
c) To prevent illegal copying of software
d) To allow secure copying of software

Q6   Which of the following is true regarding the age or gender of learners?

a) Older learners require more support than younger learners
b) Younger learners are more confident in the use of ICT than older learners
c) Female learners have more difficulty using ICT
d) None of the above

Q7   Which of the following can help to prevent viruses?

a) Regular defragmentation of the hard drive
b) Not opening attachments from unknown sources
c) Using a broadband connection
d) None of the above

Q8   What is SENDA?

a) Revision to the Disability Discrimination Act to exclude education
b) Special Educational Needs and Disability Act
c) Revision to the Disability Discrimination Act to include education
d) Statement of Educational Needs and Disabilities

Q9   Which of the following are subject to the Copyright, Designs and Patents Act (1988)? (Select all that apply.)

a) Hacking into computers
b) Illegal copying of software
c) Illegal file sharing
d) Distribution of viruses

Q10   Which of the following are subject to the Computer Misuse Act (1990)? (Select all that apply.)

   a) Hacking into computers
   b) Illegal copying of software
   c) Illegal file sharing
   d) Distribution of viruses

Q11   Identify whether the following are true or false.

   a) Broadband is available throughout the entire United Kingdom.   True/False
   b) Search engine results are not screened for unsuitable links.   True/False
   c) Organisational policies regarding ICT do not apply to learners.   True/False
   d) ICT legislation does not apply within educational organisations.   True/False
   e) A virus can only be activated by opening an e-mail.   True/False
   f) Phishing e-mails look very different to genuine e-mails.   True/False
   g) Organisational settings may not prevent access to unsuitable websites.   True/False
   h) When you purchase a music CD you own the copyright.   True/False
   i) Broadband is not the only way to access the internet.   True/False
   j) Under 18s cannot be prosecuted for illegal copying.   True/False

Q12   Consider the case study below and answer the questions that follow.

Twenty learners have enrolled for a new course and as part of the initial assessment it has been identified that the group comprises a mix of abilities and four of these have only basic ICT skills because of lack of access to ICT at home. All of the learners are 16–18 years old and will be required to use a computer within lessons and to create coursework.

   a) What can be done at the start of the course to reassure the learners with basic ICT skills?
   b) What facilities or support exists to help these learners?
   c) What can be done to ensure that the four learners are not disadvantaged during activities?

Q13   Consider the case study below and answer the questions that follow.

A group of mothers whose children go to a local school are attending an adult learning class. The parents are aged between 20 and 40 and live in an area of social disadvantage. The course aims to develop literacy, language and numeracy skills. The majority of the learners have little or no ICT skills. However, during initial discussions they have said that they would like to develop skills in this area so that they can help their children with homework and look to gain employment in the future.

   a) What issues and barriers may exist with this group of learners?
   b) In what ways could ICT be incorporated into the teaching of numeracy skills?
   c) In what ways could ICT be incorporated into the teaching of literacy skills?
   d) In what ways could ICT be incorporated into the teaching of language skills?

Q14   Consider the case study below and answer the questions that follow.

A short course is to be offered to teach senior citizens e-mail and ICT skills. Initial assessment and discussion has identified that one of the learners has a disability and has limited mobility in both hands and this needs to be considered when planning the course.

a) Which Act requires you to make reasonable adjustments for this learner?

b) In terms of using a computer, what barriers could the limited mobility have for this learner?

c) Can you suggest ways of supporting this learner via use of appropriate software or hardware?

Q15 You have been asked to teach a module on an Access to Higher Education course. As part of this module, learners are asked to examine the use of ICT in their chosen career and have asked you for advice. For this question you should consider each area and explain how and why ICT is used in the specified profession.

a) Primary school teacher

b) Solicitor

c) Nurse

d) Journalist

Q16 Complete the sentences by using words or phrases from the list below.

trojan, cookies, malware, web browsers, spyware

......................is the general term used to refer to software created with malicious intent.

A .... is software that appears innocent, for example a game or computer utility, but ultimately is created with malicious intent.

.... is software that can be inadvertently installed on a computer and monitors the user's actions.

............enable user's details to be recalled when revisiting a website. They may be disabled within some............

A SUMMARY OF KEY POINTS

In this chapter we have looked at the following key points.

> **A range of personal and social factors that can influence ICT learning and development.**

> **Legal issues and implications of ICT use.**

> **Possible barriers to learning and ways to overcome these in order to provide an inclusive learning environment.**

REFERENCES AND FURTHER READING REFERENCES AND FURTHER READING

Websites

British Dyslexia Association (2009) Frequently asked questions – what is dyslexia?:
   www.bdadyslexia.org.uk/faq.html#q1

Office of Public Sector Information. Information regarding UK Acts of Parliament:
   www.opsi.gov.uk/acts

Open University (2006) Making your teaching inclusive. Information about wide range of assistive technologies:
   www.open.ac.uk/inclusiveteaching/pages/inclusive-teaching/assistive-technologies.php

5
ICT tools

By the end of this chapter you should be able to:

- identify uses for office tools in your teaching role;
- apply formatting within a range of office tools;
- use standard features of word processors, spreadsheets, databases and presentation graphics software.

This chapter relates to the following minimum core requirements:

A2 Develop own confidence in selecting and using ICT skills in various situations.

 Develop own personal ICT skills and knowledge.

B Developing and presenting information.

This chapter also contributes to the following LLUK Standards:

BK5.1, BP5.1.

In order to meet minimum core requirements you will be required to effectively use a range of computer-related software. Office tools are one category of software that will be particularly relevant. These tools will enable you to write letters and reports, maintain learner records, design handouts and create professional presentations for use within the classroom.

Key information

HINTS AND TIPS

Office tools are frequently provided as an integrated application – this means that a number of tools are provided together, for example, word processors, spreadsheets, presentation tools and databases. A distinct advantage of this is that when you have mastered many of the standard functions in one application, you are able to apply what you have learned to another.

Consider word processing software, which can be used to create handouts, letters and reports. These can be enhanced by using toolbar buttons to change the text size, appearance, colour and position. All of these same buttons can be used within spread-sheet and presentation software with the same result.

Frequently used buttons – Windows toolbars

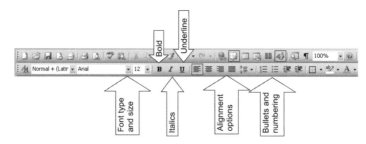

Spreadsheets

Spreadsheets comprise a grid made up of columns and rows. Columns are identified by a letter and rows identified by a number; therefore any location on the grid (a cell) can be identified by a combination of the column letter and row number. Thus the cell in column C, row 6 is given the identifier C6. This way of identifying a cell has many advantages and means that calculations can be performed easily and effectively.

Identifying cell locations

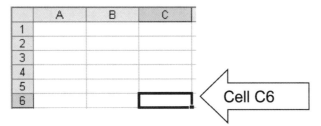

Cell C6

Many teachers use spreadsheets to track student assignments and can use input data to work out averages, highest scores and even display results graphically to identify trends. Manipulation of the basic data is achieved by using formulae and functions.

Using formulas and functions

A formula can comprise cell references, numbers and operators (+, -, *, / etc). However, in order to distinguish them from numbers or text they always start with an equals sign. Consider the example below:

EXAMPLE

A group of students have taken a test in two parts, both marked out of 50. For monitoring purposes these results are combined in this Excel spreadsheet. The spreadsheet can do this for the first student if the formula =B2+C2 is entered into cell D2.

	A	B	C	D
1	STUDENT	TEST 1	TEST 2	TOTAL
2	Sue Gwynne	32	41	
3	Patricia Brown	36	33	
4	James Roberts	39	36	
5	Jaswinder Singh	45	34	
6	Steven Williams	31	48	
7				

=B2+C2

By using the range of operators available it is possible to create increasingly complex formulas, however, the use of functions can save considerable effort.

Functions are formulas that have been created for you. As with formulas, they begin with an equals sign. After the equals sign is the name of the function, for example, the AVERAGE function can be used to calculate the average of a range of cells. The function also requires an argument, that is to say a set of values that it will use.

EXAMPLE

A function can be used to calculate the average result for each student following their 4 tests.

	A	B	C	D	E	F
1	**STUDENT**	**TEST 1**	**TEST 2**	**TEST 3**	**TEST 4**	**AVERAGE**
2	Sue Gwynne	76	74	70	82	
3	Patricia Brown	52	63	65	55	
4	James Roberts	43	51	45	48	
5	Jaswinder Singh	84	80	73	68	
6	Steven Williams	65	35	58	62	
7						

=AVERAGE(B2:E2)

All functions begin with = and follow with the function name and the range (B2:E2) enclosed in brackets. Spreadsheet applications have a wide range of functions available including MAX and MIN which give the maximum and minimum values and SUM which totals the values in a range.

Presentation software

Presentation software, for example PowerPoint, can be an effective way of incorporating ICT into lessons, providing a slideshow for learners to view. Presentations comprise one or more slides which can be viewed in a chosen order, with the range of slide types allowing the user to display text, images, graphs, tables, sound and movie clips.

Slides

Slides are the foundation of presentations and by default a title slide is provided when a new presentation is created. Additional slides are inserted using the *Insert – New slide* option from the menu bar, the user can then select the required slide type. An array of choices as to the slide layout exists as can be seen below:

Examples of slide layout

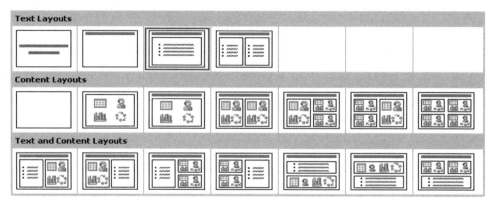

Design

Slide background and colour is an important consideration. This is referred to as the *design*. By default, once selected this is used on all slides in the current presentation.

HINTS AND TIPS

The choice of background should be made carefully to ensure that those viewing the show can distinguish the text and images clearly. Presentation software comes with a variety of built-in options and can be selected by choosing **Format – Slide Design** from the menu bar.

Entering and editing text

Entering the text is straightforward, simply click into the required area and type. The software will automatically choose an appropriate text size. If you choose a slide with title and text it will automatically add bullet points to emphasise the key points that you make.

Slide transition

Slide transition is the way that slides appear and can include options to spin, have blinds effect or even have a chequerboard effect.

HINTS AND TIPS

Recommended practice is to select one option and use it throughout the presentation – otherwise, learners will spend too much time focusing on the transitions, rather than the content.

Custom animation

Whereas slide transition involves the whole slide, custom animation is how and when individual elements of a slide appear. These may be preset or controlled at the click of a mouse. To add or amend animation, select *Slideshow – Custom Animation*. A variety of options exist for animating slide elements, including allowing text to fly in from varying directions or have the appearance of diamonds.

Databases

Spreadsheets can be useful in maintaining learner records; however, for large numbers of learners, it may be more effective to use a database. Many educational establishments use databases to store staff and learner records.

A database comprises one or more tables. Each table holds a set of related records, for example student details and assignment results. To ensure integrity of the data, one field in each table is usually assigned as a unique identifier and is referred to as a primary key. In a student details table this could be the student Id number and means that only one record with that number is permitted in the table.

In the table below, created in Microsoft Access and seen in design view, the primary key is denoted by the key symbol to the left of the field name.

Access – Design view showing primary key

	Field Name	Data Type	
🔑	Student Id Number	Number	
	First Name	Text	
	Last Name	Text	
	Contact Number	Text	

Each field required needs to be created in design view and allocated a data type. Once this has been done, data can be entered and displayed in datasheet view:

Access – datasheet view

Fields

Student Id Number	First Name	Last Name	Contact Number
1	Sue	Gwynne	01772 634765
2	Patricia	Brown	01772 678987
3	James	Roberts	05567 234897
4	Jaswinder	Singh	03787 564989
5	Steven	Williams	05567 234897
0			

Records

Forms
Forms are an easy way to enter data into a database table and can be quickly created using a wizard. They remove the need for the user to have direct access to the database tables. The form below demonstrates this.

Access – example of form

Student Contact

Student Id Number	1
First Name	Sue
Last Name	Gwynne
Contact Number	01772 634765

Record: 1 of 5

Queries
Databases are designed with the aim of storing hundreds, even thousands of records, therefore a way of retrieving data from the database is required. This is the role of the query which can be created using the wizard or in design view.

The query can be used in combination with a range of operators including those shown below:

    >   Greater than
    >= Greater than or equal to
    <   Less than
    <= Less than or equal to
    =   Equal to
    <> Not equal to

EXAMPLE

To retrieve records for those students with student number greater than 2, the following query would be used.

Query1 : Select Query

Student Contact

```
*
Student Id Number
First Name
Last Name
Contact Number
```

Field:	Student Id Number	First Name	Last Name	Contact Number	
Table:	Student Contact	Student Contact	Student Contact	Student Contact	
Sort:					
Show:	✓	✓	✓	✓	☐
Criteria:	>2				
or:					

Key questions

Q1 A word processor can be used to:

a) perform calculations
b) create a slideshow
c) create letters and reports
d) enter, sort and query data

Q2 A formula is:

a) a function
b) an area of a spreadsheet
c) an instruction to perform a calculation
d) essential in a spreadsheet

Q3 An argument is:

a) part of a function
b) a type of spreadsheet
c) a complex function
d) an essential part of a function

Q4 To change the way that a slide appears in a presentation, you need to change the:

a) animation
b) transition
c) file type
d) hyperlink

Q5 Which of the following can be used in a slideshow? (Select all that apply.)

a) Images
b) Text
c) Sound clips
d) Movie clips

Q6 In a database, data is stored in:

a) records
b) columns
c) rows
d) objects

Q7 A primary key:

a) allows access to the database
b) is a unique identifier
c) restricts access to the database
d) is the same as a foreign key

Q8 In a word processor, which of the following will allow more text to be shown? (Select all that apply.)

a) Decrease the size of the margins
b) Increase the margin sizes
c) Reduce the font size
d) Decrease the font size

Q9 Which of the following could be used to add together the values in cells A1 and A9?

a) =SUM(A1:A9)
b) =A1*A9
c) =A1+A9
d) =SUM(A1) + SUM (A9)

Q10 A slideshow can be advanced:

a) automatically
b) manually
c) automatically and manually
d) via use of a password

Q11 Match the following file types to their extension:

1. .xls   A. Presentation
2. .doc   B. Spreadsheet
3. .pps   C. Word processor
4. .mdb   D. Database

Q12 Match the purpose with the most appropriate font type:

1. Used for typing a letter   A. 32
2. Used for a slideshow heading   B. 12

3. Used for slideshow text   C. 8
4. Used for a header or footer   D. 26

Q13 Circle the correct choice in the statements below.

a) A *spreadsheet/database* is the best way to store large amounts of student data.
b) When using a word processor the page size *may/must* be A4.
c) You *need to/need not* purchase each of the different office applications separately.
d) You *should/should not* use lots of different colours in a slideshow.
e) When using a spellchecker you *do/do not* have to worry about your spelling.
f) A word processor *is/is not* suitable for images.

Q14 The following questions relate to the spreadsheet shown below:

	A	B	C	D
1	Department	Target 2007	Target 2008	Target Increase
2	Lifelong Learning	256	278	
3	Languages	134	166	
4	Early Years	160	220	
5	Health and Social Care	155	198	
6	Skills for Life	234	310	
7			Average Target Increase	
8			Minimum Target Increase	
9			Maximum Target Increase	

a) Which formula should be entered into cell D2 to calculate the target increase?
   (i)   =C2-B2
   (ii) =B2-C2
   (iii) =B2*C2
   (iv) =SUM(C2-B2)

b) Consider the text in cell C7. How is the text formatted and aligned?
   (i)   Italics, left aligned
   (ii) Bold, left aligned
   (iii) Bold, right aligned.

c) What function should be entered into cell D7 to calculate the average target increase?
   (i)   =AVERAGE(D2:D6)
   (ii) = AVG
   (iii) =AVERAGE(D7)

d) What function should be entered into cell D9 to calculate the maximum target increase?
   (i)   = MAXIMUM(D2:D6)
   (ii) =MAX(D8)
   (iii) = MAX (D2:D6)

Q15 The following questions relate to the database shown below.

Student Number	Assignment Number	Hand in Date	Result
MN4356	1	01/11/1991	67
MN7657	1	02/11/2009	46
MN8909	1	02/11/2009	0
MN7812	1	03/11/2009	75

Table1 : Table

a) What would be the most appropriate choice of data type for the student number field?
   (i)   Text
   (ii) Number, single
   (iii) Number, integer

b) What would be the most appropriate choice of data type for the result field?
   (i)   Number, single
   (ii) Number, integer
   (iii) Number, double

c) Which field would be most appropriate to use as a primary key?
   (i)   Result
   (ii) Student Number
   (iii) Hand in Date

d) When creating a query, the criteria to view results of at least 45 would be specified as:
   (i)   >=45
   (ii) <=45
   (iii) >45

e) To create a query to find out which students handed their assignments in after the hand-in date of 2nd November, what criteria would need to be specified?
   (i)   =02/11/09
   (ii) <> 01/11/09
   (iii) >02/11/09

Q16 The following questions relate to the poster shown below

Maths Taster

Various days and times

Free

Monday   9am – 12noon
Wednesday   1pm – 4pm
Saturday   8am – 11am

Contact Grace on *678345* to reserve your place!

Complete the sentences by choosing the correct phrases from below:
bold, italics left aligned, centred, autoshapes, tabs

a) The explosion image has been created by using ....

b) The heading is .... and...

c) The best way to ensure that the course times are aligned is by using ....

d) The days are ....

e) The telephone number is shown in ....

Q17 The following questions relate to the slides displayed below.

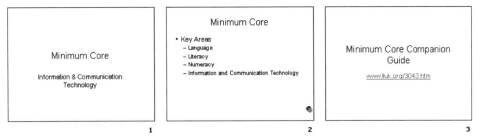

a) Identify the title slide(s).
   (i)   Slide 1
   (ii) Slide 1 and slide 3
   (iii) Slide 2

b) The slides are displayed in which view?
   (i)   Slide view
   (ii) Outline view
   (iii) Slide sorter view

c) Which slide contains a sound clip?
   (i)   Slide 1
   (ii) Slide 2
   (iii) Slide 3

d) Slide 3 contains a hyperlink, what is the purpose of this particular hyperlink?
   (i)   To display a website
   (ii) To open a file
   (iii) To play a movie clip

Q18 This question considers printing options within office software.

a) You have a spreadsheet that takes up just over one page when printed. What action can you take?

b) You issue slideshow handouts to your learners with four slides to a page, though your learners have commented that they don't have anywhere to write their notes. How can you overcome this?

c) You want to print a copy of your slideshow handouts to check their appearance, though do not have much coloured ink in your printer. What option exists to reduce the coloured ink that you use?

d) You are printing 20 copies of a presentation, though have noticed that you need to manually sort the pages as 20 copies of page 1 come out together, then 20 copies of page 2 and finally 20 copies of page 3. What option will remove the need to manually sort the pages?

e) You have a large document comprising over 50 pages and want to get a clear idea of how it will look when printed, but want to save ink. How can you do this?

A SUMMARY OF KEY POINTS

In this chapter we have looked at the following key points.

> **Any teaching role will require a range of skills in the use of office tools including word processors, databases, spreadsheets and presentation graphics.**

> **Use of these tools will prove invaluable for writing letters and reports, maintaining learner records, designing handouts and creating professional presentations for use within the classroom.**

> **You will now be able to use the standard features of the range of office tools for a variety of purposes essential in your teaching role, not only in supporting and enhancing learning but also for monitoring and record keeping purposes.**

REFERENCES AND FURTHER READING REFERENCES AND FURTHER READING

Cox, J, Frye, C and Preppernau, J (2007) *Microsoft® home office and student 2007 step by step.* Microsoft Press

Websites

Microsoft Office online training: http://office.microsoft.com/en-gb/training/default.aspx

6
Purposeful use of ICT

By the end of this chapter you should be able to:

- **identify the range of technology available to support and enhance teaching;**
- **analyse the appropriateness of ICT in different learning contexts;**
- **suggest ways of using ICT to enhance teaching and learning.**

This chapter relates to the following minimum core requirements:

A2 Purposeful use of ICT.

This chapter also contributes to the following LLUK Standards:

BK5.1, BP5.1, BK5.2, CP2.1, CK3.5, CP3.5, CP4.2, DP1.2.

The development of your own ICT skills should naturally lead to developed confidence in supporting learners and incorporating ICT into your lessons to enhance the learning experience. This chapter will consider ways in which ICT can be utilised for both of these reasons.

Key information

The wide range of ICT technologies available offers many opportunities for incorporating ICT into your teaching, be it through the use of personal computers, learning environments, camcorders, cameras and even mobile phones. By using these technologies, learning can be enhanced and learners can be further motivated.

Blended learning and e-learning are two phrases commonly used when referring to the use of ICT in the classroom. Whereas e-learning was traditionally used to refer to purely electronic learning, the blended learning approach combines traditional teaching with e-learning to give a combined approach.

HINTS AND TIPS

A common mistake that teachers make when looking to incorporate ICT into their teaching is to try to find *any* way of using it, rather than, as the chapter heading suggests, making it purposeful, engaging and relevant to the group of learners they are teaching. Consider a group of senior citizens in a residential setting. It would be inappropriate to get them to send text messages as a way of communication if they have little or no knowledge of the devices. However, if they were keen to use e-mail to keep in contact with family this could be a more appropriate technology to use in terms of motivation.

One way of starting to incorporate ICT into your teaching is to consider what you currently do and how this can be enhanced, both for yourself and your learners by adopting an ICT-based solution.

Learning environments

A virtual learning environment (VLE) may be available within your organisation to support your learners. A VLE comprises a range of facilities that can be accessed on-site or remotely via an internet connection. Moodle and Blackboard are two VLEs that you may be familiar with and enable teachers to provide a range of learning resources, discussion forums and activities for student use. By placing classroom resources on a VLE, learners can study remotely or have access to learning resources when they are unable to attend.

Other advantages of VLEs are reduced cost to the organisation and also the environmental impact. Rather than having to print out resources and learner handouts, the learners can be directed to the VLE and print only what they require.

Mobile phones and video conferencing

Many learners have use of a mobile phone, which teachers can use as a learning resource. This doesn't require a huge financial input and therefore can be relatively simple to incorporate. In addition, learners find it a refreshing change not to be asked to switch off their phones. Mobile phones can be used to replace questioning as an assessment tool and learners can undertake a task and feed back to the tutor via use of a text message or bluetooth facility. The range of facilities available on many phones, including calculators, organisers, sound recording and camera facilities, means that they can be used in many innovative ways.

EXAMPLE

A step beyond the use of mobile phones is the use of video calls, using facilities such as Skype, which can be used in conjunction with a webcam. Video calls can be used to introduce guest speakers to a class with greater ease, less cost and resource use than using a personal visit, yet add a novel element to a lesson.

Multimedia and online media sources

Multimedia is the term used to represent the use of a variety of media including images, audio and video. The ability to view DVDs, on-line videos, interactive CD ROMs, radio and television programmes via a personal computer has led to an increase in their use in teaching. Multimedia has the advantage that it appeals to the range of learning styles.

Online resources need to be evaluated, particularly regarding the accuracy if acquired from a source that is not subject to any form of screening and also in respect to copyright issues (see Chapter 8).

Interactive whiteboards

Interactive whiteboards are now widely available in colleges and educational organisations. However, they are frequently used just as a white screen for the projector to display upon. The combination of an interactive white board and projector can be a powerful tool, with learners being able to use a pen or their finger to move objects, answer questions and actively interact with the board.

An advantage of using some interactive white boards is the ability to write on the board with a pen, as with a traditional board, but be able to save and print the writing to provide the teacher or learners with a permanent copy.

Image capturing devices

The evolution of image capturing devices has led to digital cameras, camcorders, mobile phones and personal digital assistants (PDAs) with built-in cameras. The cost of these devices has reduced considerably in recent years making them more widely available in education.

EXAMPLE

Cameras and image capturing devices can be used for many purposes, including photographing learners' work for exam evidence purposes and photographing diagrams drawn on a traditional whiteboard. Camcorders can be used to record and play back drama performances, to record interview simulations, debates and group interactions and consequently to help learners identify development areas.

Personal computers and software

Personal computers are now such an integral part of society that it is only natural that they are used in education. Many awarding bodies insist that learners' assignments are word processed if they are to be accepted. It is essential, therefore, that both teachers and learners are competent in the use of personal computers and related software.

Within the classroom environment, computers can be used for a range of learner-centred activities, including research, creation of presentations, posters, and assignment tasks.

EXAMPLE

Traditional office software, discussed in Chapter 5 can be used effectively within the classroom. Spreadsheet software can be used to create interactive quizzes; word processing software can be used to create text boxes, which can be manipulated by a mouse or via a whiteboard, and learners can use presentations software to create a slide show.

HINTS AND TIPS

It would be easy to assume that all teachers have access to an array of technology. However, this is often not the case, especially for those who teach in community centres, libraries and other locations. In these cases, a laptop with a mobile broadband connection can be used in order to access the internet.

Resource banks

A major cost- and time-saving facility exists in the form of resource banks. These resource banks comprise ICT-based teaching and learning resources that have been created by others and are available in a wide range of topics and age ranges. In terms of quality of these resources, evaluation is always recommended, but some resource banks have the facility for users to award a rating based on their opinion to assist in making your judgement.

Graphics calculators

Graphics calculators are relevant to learners undertaking courses with a mathematical content and have a wide range of functions and uses, including graph plotting, equation solving and trigonometry. Whilst many do require a time investment to learn to use them, they can help develop learners' technological skills and are highly portable.

Key questions

Q1   What is blended learning?

a) Using a wide range of technologies within a session
b) Learning that does not involve the use of ICT
c) Using ICT in combination with a traditional teaching approach

Q2   What is e-learning?

a) Electronic learning
b) Effective learning
c) Efficient learning

Q3   What is a VLE?

a) Virtual Learning Environment
b) Visual Learning Experience
c) Virtual Learning Experience

Q4   Which of the following are features of a VLE? (Select all that apply.)

a) Free peer to peer telephone calls
b) Discussion facilities
c) Hyperlinks to websites
d) On-line tests

Q5   Which of the following could prevent a learner using a VLE from home?

a) No knowledge of computer programming
b) No internet access
c) No access to a mobile phone
d) No access to a webcam

Q6   What is multimedia?

a) Use of a range of technologies during a lesson
b) A combination of different media
c) A specific format of personal computers

Q7   Which of the following are advantages of multimedia?

a) Appealing to a range of learning styles
b) Cost
c) No need to consider copyright

Q8   Which of the following are disadvantages of resource banks?

a) High cost
b) Some areas may not have resources available
c) Unknown quality of resources

Q9   Which of the following are advantages of Skype technology?

a) Free broadband connection
b) No need for a webcam for video calls
c) Free Skype to Skype video calls

Q10   How can you ensure purposeful use of ICT?

a) Ensure that you use it in every lesson
b) Ensure that you create all of the resources that you use
c) Ensure learners do not have to share resources
d) Consider the appropriateness of ICT and how it can enhance learning

The following questions will ask you to consider how you can use ICT solutions for the benefit of both yourself and your learners.

Q11   You have a group of learners who attend college every other week. To check their progress you telephone them individually. This can be time consuming, because they often do not answer and you need to ring them several times in order to get a response. How can ICT be utilised to help with this task?

Q12   You often use a pair matching exercise, whereby learners have to match the Act of Parliament with the contents. The task is currently undertaken with two sets of cards, one containing details of the act, the other set the contents. How can you adapt this task to incorporate ICT?

Q13   You have recently had a lesson observation by your tutor who has identified two developmental areas. The first suggestion is to try to incorporate ICT into your session and the second is to check learning more effectively at the end of the session. The only ICT available to you are the learners' mobile phones. How can these be used to check learning more effectively?

Q14   You teach embroidery in a community centre and have limited access to ICT. However, you have recently inherited a laptop computer, which has internet access via mobile broadband. How can this computer be used to enhance the group's learning?

Q15   Identify whether the following are true or false.

a) Mobile broadband cannot be used with a laptop computer.   True/False
b) Personal computers are the most effective way of using ICT in teaching. True/False
c) ICT is inappropriate for use in community settings.   True/False
d) ICT can be used to enhance teaching and motivate learners.   True/False
e) Blended learning involves the use of ICT.   True/False
f) Poorly used ICT can demotivate learners.   True/False
g) A VLE can be accessed remotely.   True/False
h) Skype requires an internet connection.   True/False
i) Multimedia is mainly relevant to visual learners.   True/False
j) Text written on an interactive whiteboard can be saved.   True/False

Q16   Complete the sentences by using words from the list below:

resource banks, community, bluetooth, evaluated, mobile phones, resources, time, mobile, internet, text, classroom

.... broadband can be used when an .... connection is not available and is particularly relevant for use in .... settings.

.... can have many different uses in the........... The........... and .... facilities can be used to send messages between the group and to/from the teacher.

.... are depositories of ....created by others and can save .... compared to creating your own. However, they should be .... prior to use.

Q17 For each of the resources/technologies listed below, give suggestions as to how they could be used to enhance learning in the lifelong learning sector.

a) Mobile phones
b) Personal computers
c) Digital cameras
d) Video cameras
e) Video conferencing

Q18 For the scenarios below, consider why the use of ICT could have a negative impact on learning, giving suggestions as to how this could be overcome and learning enhanced.

a) A lecturer wants to use a digital camera in class and nominates one person to photograph the group's work.
b) Learners on a psychology course are sent to the learning resource centre to conduct independent web research on their forthcoming assignment.
c) A lecturer asks learners to text her if they have any questions before the next session.
d) A lecturer asks the class to divide themselves into four groups, tasking the groups to prepare a slideshow presentation to the rest of the class.
e) A lecturer has recently acquired a remote keyboard and mouse, though uses just the mouse to advance slides in his presentation.

A SUMMARY OF KEY POINTS

In this chapter we have looked at the following key points.

> **The purposeful use of ICT.**

> **A range of technology has been identified that is available to the teacher and learners.**

> **The appropriateness of these technologies in different contexts, with suggestions as to how ICT can be implemented in ways that can enhance teaching and learning.**

REFERENCES AND FURTHER READING REFERENCES AND FURTHER READING

Hill, C (2008) *Teaching with e-learning in the lifelong learning sector.* 2nd edition. Exeter: Learning Matters

Websites

British Educational Communications and Technology Agency: http://feandskills.becta.org.uk/
Times Educational Supplement – Resources: www.tes.co.uk/resourcehub.aspx

7
ICT systems

By the end of this chapter you should be able to:

- **manage Windows settings and properties;**
- **identify and use range of storage media;**
- **use Windows Explorer to create folders, copy, move, rename and delete files;**
- **perform basic troubleshooting.**

This chapter relates to the following minimum core requirements:

B   Using ICT systems

This chapter also contributes to the following LLUK Standards:

CK3.5, CP3.5, BK5.1, BP5.1

Effective use of ICT systems, whether as a tool to support teaching and learning or to assist in your professional role outside of the classroom, requires skills to effectively use and change computer settings. The ability to manage files, change settings, manage a variety of media and to undertake basic troubleshooting correctly are essential. This chapter will consider these areas.

Key information

Windows settings and properties

Whilst being able to use office tools is a key skill you will need to master, you will also need to manage system settings including screen resolution, appearance and background. These settings can be revised via the display option within the control panel.

Screen resolution refers to the number of pixels on the screen and is represented by two values, one for width and one for height. By selecting a higher resolution, for example 1024 x 768, the size of icons is decreased and by selecting a lower resolution such as 800 x 600, the size of icons is increased. Changing resolution settings is one way of supporting learners' individual needs – they may find it difficult to use the computer on high resolution setting.

Many users like to change the desktop background in order to personalise the computer and can select from a range of images and even choose their own photograph. This setting can be changed by selecting desktop within the display option.

Storage media

The range of storage media available has evolved considerably over recent years. Not so long ago, floppy disks were one of the main forms of storage for learners and teachers, but they were low capacity and susceptible to damage by magnets in a variety of forms, including mobile phones. The use of the pen drive, or USB memory stick, is now a popular portable option. The capacity of pen drives can vary greatly from less than 1GB to 8GB and beyond and is an excellent way of storing teaching resources in a portable format.

HINTS AND TIPS

Pen drives are connected to the computer via a USB slot and should always be removed safely, rather than just unplugging from the computer. If you examine the screen at the bottom right of the computer you will find a notification area that forms part of the taskbar.

Windows – Task bar notification area

Safely remove hardware

To remove your device safely you should locate the icon for the memory stick and click, selecting safely remove hardware when prompted. This will help to prevent accidental loss of some or all of your data.

Compact disks can be used for long-term storage and are available in two types, CD-R and CD-RW. CD-R disks can be used only once, whereas CD-RW can be erased and used again. CDs usually have a capacity of 700MB. Some CD drives take both types of disks, though it would be wise to check before purchasing.

Digital Versatile Disks (DVDs) are also available in rewriteable and non-rewritable options, and have greater storage capacity than CDs. In the case of DVDs, they usually have a capacity of 4.7GB. They can only be read in DVD drives.

Storage capacity of media

Media	Capacity
Floppy disk	1.44MB
CD-R/RW	700MB
DVD-R/W	4.7GB
USB memory	Up to 8GB and beyond

HINTS AND TIPS

Storage is measured in Megabytes and Gigabytes. 1GB is equivalent to 1024 MB.

Protecting storage media

An important consideration in the use of storage media is safe storage and protection from damage. They should be kept dry, and in the case of CDs and DVDs should be protected from scratching or anything that might damage the surface of the disks.

File management

Use of a computer in conjunction with a range of software will, no doubt, lead to the creation of a number of documents and files that you will need to organise. This is the role of file management software, in the case of windows, this is Windows Explorer.

Windows Explorer provides the user with the ability to copy, move, delete and rename files. Folders can be created to ensure efficient organisation of files and to ensure that you can find that all important file when needed.

A folder   **Files**

DTLLS

BEHAVIOUR week 2

Developing Your EI

Windows Explorer can be accessed by right clicking on the Start menu and selecting explore or by using the keyboard shortcut which is found by pressing and holding the Windows key and pressing the letter E on your keyboard.

When you open Windows Explorer, you will see that the screen is split into two distinct parts or panes – the left pane displays all the drives and folders that the computer has access to and the right pane displays the contents of whatever is selected in the left pane.

Copying and moving files
Files can be moved easily by dragging them to the required folder, whereas to copy a file you can right click and drag to the required folder, selecting **Copy Here** if prompted.

Renaming
You may find that you want to change the name of a file or folder to make it clearer what it contains. By right clicking on the file or folder and selecting **Rename**, the name will become blocked in blue, to change it you just need to type the new name and press enter.

Deleting
Deleting a file is very straightforward, you should just click on the file or folder that you wish to delete and either press the delete button on your keyboard or on the Windows Explorer toolbar. Be aware though that if you delete a folder, you also delete the contents.

Windows Explorer – Contents of My Pictures Folder

EXAMPLE

To sort the files in ascending order of size, click on the Size heading. Clicking again will sort them in descending order.

Basic troubleshooting

As with any technology, the time may come when your computer doesn't perform as expected and you don't know what to do to put it right. This is where basic troubleshooting comes in. Having the knowledge to solve such problems will save you time and enable you to work more efficiently.

HINTS AND TIPS

A common problem when using a computer is when it fails to respond, this is often referred to as being 'frozen'. If this happens, you can try pressing the **CTRL**, **ALT** and **DELETE** keys simultaneously. This will usually bring up the Task Manager which displays programs that are running. You should highlight the program that is not responding and click on the End Task button.

If you find that programs aren't frozen but are not working correctly, for example, in a word processor the tabs don't work or in a spreadsheet cells won't format correctly, this is when you should try shutting down and restarting the computer. This can be selected from the Start menu.

Mice, keyboards, speakers, printers and other devices connected to the computer via cables can often present a problem if they become loose, therefore if any of these devices fail to function it would be wise to first check that the appropriate cables are secure.

Printers can present with a number of problems, therefore it is worth performing some basic checks if the printer doesn't respond. You should check that paper is in the printer, that it is switched on and that the paper hasn't jammed.

Key questions

Q1   If you have a learner who has difficulty seeing the icons on screen, what can you do?

    a) Change the resolution to 1024 × 768
    b) Change the resolution to 800 × 600
    c) Change the resolution to 800 × 768
    d) Change the resolution to 1024 × 600

Q2   What is a folder?

    a) A type of icon to represent a file
    b) A way of securing files from viruses
    c) A location on a disk or computer that can contain other folders and files
    d) A location on a disk or computer that contains just files

Q3   In Windows Explorer, what happens if you click on the plus (+) symbol to the left of a folder icon?

    a) The folder is expanded to show sub folders
    b) The folder is closed
    c) Sub folders are deleted
    d) The folder is deleted

Q4   What is 1028MB, better known as?

    a) 10GB
    b) 1KB
    c) 2GB
    d) 1GB

Q5   Which of the following would be most likely to have storage capacity of 700MB?

    a) DVD-R/RW
    b) CD-R/RW
    c) USB memory stick
    d) Floppy disk

Q6   What 3 button option should you use when the computer 'freezes'?

    a) CTRL – ALT – DELETE
    b) CTRL – DELETE – ALT
    c) WINDOWS – E – DELETE
    d) CTRL – SHIFT – DELETE

Q7   When a file is copied into a folder, what happens to the original?

    a) It is deleted
    b) It is moved to the folder with the copy
    c) It remains in its original location
    d) It is saved into a copied files folder

Q8   What is a DVD?

a) Digital Video Disk
b) Desktop Versatile Disk
c) Deletable Versatile Disk
d) Digital Versatile Disk

Q9   Would you experience problems using a DVD disk in a CD drive?

a) Yes. A DVD can only be read in a DVD drive.
b) Yes. If the DVD was DVD-R.
c) No. They are completely compatible.
d) No. As long as the DVD is DVD-RW.

Q10   Which of the following disks are reusable? (Select all that apply.)

a) DVD-RW
b) CD-R
c) CD-RW
d) DVD-R

Q11   Complete the sentences regarding storage media by choosing the correct phrases from the list below:

DVDs, CDs, Floppy disks, DVD-R, CD-R, CD-RW, DVD-RW

.... generally have a storage capacity of 700MB. The reusable version is known as ...., whereas the non-reusable version is known as ....

.... generally have a storage capacity of 4.7GB. The reusable version is known as ...., whereas the non-reusable version is known as.............

.... can be corrupted by being placed near a mobile phone.

Q12   Identify whether the following are true or false.

a) The left side of Windows Explorer displays files.	True/False
b) The control panel can be launched by pressing CTRL-ALT-DELETE.	True/False
c) Clicking on the size heading in Windows Explorer will reduce the file size.	True/False
d) Using Windows Explorer is the not only way to create folders.	True/False
e) Left clicking and dragging a file to the required location is one way to copy a file.	True/False
f) Deleting a folder will not delete the contents.	True/False
g) Desktop settings can be revised via the control panel display option.	True/False
h) Folders are used to organise files in Windows Explorer.	True/False
i) Windows Explorer can be accessed via the control panel.	True/False
j) Restarting the computer will solve any software problems.	True/False

Q13   Choose one of the following media types to suit the purpose below. You may use each type only once and should use the most appropriate given the circumstances.

CD-RW, Floppy disk, USB memory, DVD

a) To store teaching resources to be accessed at home and work.
b) To save documents and transfer from an older laptop for backup purposes.
c) To save a large quantity of videos and images for use in the classroom.
d) To back up your important documents on a weekly basis.

Q14 Consider the scenarios below and decide what option you will undertake when trouble-shooting.

a) You are entering a URL in Internet Explorer, though nothing appears on screen.
b) You are trying to print a document, but nothing is coming out of the printer.
c) You are trying to close down a document, but even though you are trying to do this via the mouse and keyboard shortcuts, nothing is happening.
d) You are trying to type a letter and select the appropriate font, but this is not what appears when you type.
e) You switch the computer on in the morning and nothing happens.

Q15 For this question you should match the tools with their description.

1. Defragment   A. Saves copies of files to use if problems occur with originals
2. Scan/check disk B. Used to rollback system settings to a previous point in time
3. System Restore   C. Rearranging files on the hard disk to improve performance
4. Backup   D. Searches for unwanted files to create space on the hard disk
5. Disk Clean up   E. Searches for errors on a hard disk

Q16 The following questions relate to the screen shot reproduced below:

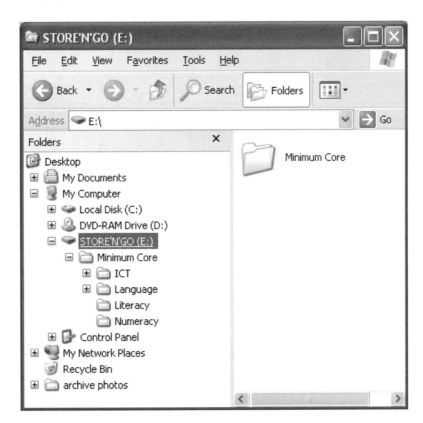

a) What letter is used to represent the selected disk?
b) What happens when the user clicks on the plus (+) symbol to the left of the folder name?

c) What happens when the user clicks on the minus (-) symbol to the left of the folder name?

d) What are the names of the visible sub folders within the Minimum Core folder?

e) How many of the sub folders contain further folders?

f) How can the user find out what space is remaining on the highlighted disk?

e) How can the entire contents of the disk be erased?

A SUMMARY OF KEY POINTS

In this chapter we have looked at the following key points.

> **The effective use of ICT systems.**

> **The ability to change display settings in order to personalise Windows.**

> **Windows Explorer has been identified as an essential tool to manage files and folders.**

> **Should problems arise when using your computer, you will now be better informed and be able to undertake basic troubleshooting.**

REFERENCES AND FURTHER READING REFERENCES AND FURTHER READING

Gookin, D (2007) *PCs for dummies.* 11th edition. Chichester: John Wiley & Sons

8
Finding, selecting and exchanging information

By the end of this chapter you should be able to:

- use Boolean operators to conduct electronic searches;
- access and evaluate websites with regards to authority, bias and currency;
- identify the features of e-mail applications.

This chapter relates to the following minimum core requirements:

A2 Essential Characteristics of ICT.

B   Finding, selecting and exchanging information.

This chapter also contributes to the following LLUK Standards:

BK3.5, BP3.5, BP5.2, CP1.1, CK4.1.

The ability for a teacher to be able to locate and evaluate information and subject resources is important. Although libraries will always play a key role in this, the ability to use the web for searching and locating information is an essential skill for a busy teacher. This chapter will develop and assess your skills in this area.

Key information

HINTS AND TIPS

The internet is a massive network of computers, a part of which is the world wide web – billions of pages of information which have been created by a wide range of people, organisations and educational establishments. Anyone with a little know-how and a computer with an internet connection can create their own website with relative ease.

Given that web pages can be created so easily, how can a user ascertain the validity of pages they locate? As a teacher it is essential that you do this with any information that you plan to use to develop your own and learners' knowledge. This is the role of evaluation, whereby you consider the evidence provided in terms of authority, bias and currency.

Authority

The first stage of evaluation usually involves finding out about who has created the article – who are they and what authority do they have in the area in which they are writing?

Often, a web page can provide information about the author either explicitly or implicitly. This can be provided by examining the name of the website, or examining the page(s) to see what author information is given. Does the author provide details regarding their experience, qualification or status in this area?

Bias

A website is more likely to be of value if there is evidence that the author is an expert in the area and does not have any bias towards the content. Consider the example when searching for political information – any content found on the pages of a specific political party will most probably be biased towards their own viewpoint. For this reason, when evaluating a website it is worth digging a little deeper. Find out about the person or organisation and what they represent, is there any evidence of bias?

Currency

When looking for up to date information, an important consideration is when the web page was created and whether it has been updated to reflect any recent changes in the chosen area. Often a web page will include a date last updated which can prove useful. Many sites are created and not updated and can provided an incomplete picture when trying to locate up to date information.

Searching

Given the size of the web, an effective way of searching for and locating information is required. This is the role of search engines and directories.

A directory is a structured way of locating information, which is created by humans into a hierarchical structure; links can be followed to locate information on a wide range of topics. The example below shows an example of the education area of a directory.

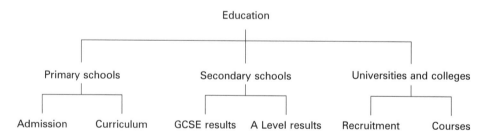

Whereas directories are useful when browsing areas of the web, search engines give the user greater freedom and allow the use of search terms to locate more specific information. Search engines often find information which has been located and organised using computer programs called web crawlers. The crawlers use information found in websites' meta tags, which is provided by creators for just this purpose and also follow links between web pages.

Popular search engines include Google and Yahoo, though many more are available and you should spend time experimenting with the different search engines to find those that best suit your individual needs.

HINTS AND TIPS

Traditionally, search engines used Boolean operators – words such as AND, OR and NOT – in conjunction with the key words used in the search. The ability to apply these operators, both for web and electronic searches, is essential. However, it should be noted that different search engines work in different ways, with some supporting Boolean operators and some not.

Operator	Purpose	Example
AND / +	To find sites containing BOTH search terms	Tower AND London
		Tower + London
OR	To find sites containing EITHER search term	Christmas OR Xmas
NOT / -	To find sites containing the first term, but NOT the second	Mermaid NOT Ariel
		Mermaid – Ariel
" "	Finds a specific phrase	"Inclusivity in education"

Wildcards can also be used to search for information, yet allow variation in the word ending. For example, if you wanted to find information on Margaret Thatcher and her policies you could use Thatcher* which would find websites about *Thatcher*, *Thatcher*ism and *Thatcher*ite, etc.

Effective use of search criteria will enable you to reduce or increase the number of 'hits' or sites that meet the specified criteria, with those that meet the criteria most closely being found near the top of the list. A word of warning though, search engines often include paid-for advertisements at the top, too, so choose carefully, taking this into consideration.

Sources of information

Whilst the world wide web is a useful source of information when combined with the use of directories and search engines, it is likely that you will also want to use other electronic information sources, which may be available from your library and include on-line journals, e-books and CD-ROMs with subject specific information. You will be able to use your searching skills in this environment too.

Journals are the traditional route for disseminating research to the academic community and as such are considered a reliable primary source, due to their having been peer reviewed. Many journals are now available on-line to subscribers and via some academic libraries.

Electronic books (e-books) are digital versions of traditional books and are becoming increasingly available to learners through academic libraries. E-books can be downloaded to a PC, a handheld device or to a specialist e-book reader.

E-mail

Having considered location of information, the next stage is to ensure that you are able to communicate information effectively to others. E-mail is a way of achieving this. It can enable rapid communication within and outside of your organisation, with learners and with others. However, use of e-mail does require that both parties have regular access to e-mail. Sending an urgent e-mail to a colleague will be of little use if they rarely access their e-mail.

A wide range of e-mail packages are available, enabling the user to compose and reply to e-mails. Some of these have the added advantage that they can be accessed on-line, from any internet-ready computer. In addition to creating and replying to e-mails, files or images can be sent along with the e-mail in the form of attachments. This is useful if learners want to sent you a draft of an assignment or if you want to send an additional handout to a learner.

Many e-mail packages include the facility to store contact details for individuals and groups. If you want to send an e-mail to a group of people, this can be achieved simply via the use of a distribution list, whereby a list of e-mails and contact details is created and grouped together to enable you to compose one e-mail and send it to all members of the group. A number of distribution lists can be created to suit individual needs and may include one per class, course or for departmental contacts.

When sending e-mails, time can be saved by inserting a signature – an automated entry that can be used on every e-mail, giving the sender's name and contact details. A different font colour, type and size are often available within this option, enabling you to create a personal signature.

HINTS AND TIPS

When sending an e-mail it is possible to send copies to others at the same time. This can be achieved using the CC or BCC field in the e-mail.

CC Sends a copy of the e-mail to the specified person in addition to the recipient

BCC Sends a copy of the e-mail to the specified person, without the recipient being aware.

EXAMPLE

You may need to send an e-mail to a learner in response to a complaint. By using the BCC field, you can reply to the complaint, but also let your manager have a copy, without making it obvious to the learner that someone else will be party to the communication.

Key questions

Q1   Identify whether the following are true or false.

a) You must use Boolean operators when searching websites.   True/False
b) Web directories are more effective than search engines for browsing topics on the web.   True/False
c) Web directories are good for accessing local information.   True/False
d) Search engines must be used to access a web page.   True/False
e) The web pages at the top of the search results list will be the most relevant.   True/False
f) Every search engine gives the same results.   True/False
g) Websites are always a reliable source of information.   True/False
h) When evaluating a website, the main consideration is how the text is presented.   True/False

i) Sending an e-mail does not require internet access.   True/False

k) An e-mail can be sent to a number of people at the same time.   True/False

Q2 Which of the following are true? (Select all that apply.)

a) Anyone can publish information on the world wide web.
b) Sites with the .com suffix are particularly reliable.
c) Each website should be considered on its own merits and evaluated accordingly.
d) You can be certain of the quality of information on a .ac or .edu website.

Q3 Complete the following sentence. Search results are:

a) Limited to 50
b) Limited to 500
c) Limited to 5000
d) Unlimited

Q4 Which of the following would be the best place to look for information regarding legislation in further education?

a) National newspapers
b) Government websites
c) Search engines
d) On-line encyclopaedias

Q5 If you choose to use an on-line resource, you:

a) Need not cite the source as the web is copyright free
b) Should cite the source as a matter of courtesy to the author
c) Must cite the source to acknowledge the author's intellectual copyright and ask permission prior to use

Q6 Which of the following is/are true about e-books?

a) e-books are only available from libraries
b) e-books are digital versions of traditional books
c) e-books are not subject to copyright
d) Text books are not available in e-book format

Q7 To send a received e-mail to another person you can use which option?

a) Compose
b) Forward
c) Reply
d) Send

Q8 A group of contacts can be organised to create a:

a) Carbon copy
b) Favourites list
c) Distribution list

Q9   Which of the following are not valid e-mail addresses? (Select all that apply.)

a) Joe.bloggs.bt
b) Joe.bloggs@bt.com
c) John.smith
d) Johnsmith@mmc.co.uk

Q10   The place to find received e-mails is:

a) Inbox
b) Drafts
c) Sent items
d) Outbox

Q11   The place to find e-mails waiting to be sent is:

a) Inbox
b) Drafts
c) Sent items
d) Outbox

Q12   Complete the sentences by choosing the correct phrases from the list below:

Speech marks (" "), many, OR, AND, may, paid, all, NOT

a) The use of Boolean operators can enhance and support electronic searches, however, they .... not be supported by .... search engines.

b) There are .... search engines, which can produce a range of different search results.

c) .... can be used to increase the number of hits when searching electronically, whereas .... and .... are used to reduce the number of hits.

d) Complete phrases can be searched for via the use of .... , however, they can have limited use unless used carefully and may results in too few hits,

e) When a list of results is presented following a search, it is important to be aware of the sponsored links which have been .... for by an advertiser.

Q13   A search using "Curriculum Design Stenhouse" will result in which of the following?

a) Pages about Stenhouse and curriculum design.
b) Pages containing the phrase "Curriculum Design Stenhouse".

Q14   If you wanted to search for pages related to humanism and the humanistic approach, which would be the best search criteria?

a) Humanism AND humanistic
b) humanis*

Q15   If you wanted to search for pages to assist in writing a literature review, which would be the best search criteria?

a) literature OR review
b) literature AND review

Q16 If you wanted to locate information about psychoanalysis but didn't want to include Freud, which would be the best search criteria?

a) Freud NOT psychoanalysis
b) psychoanalysis NOT Freud

Q17 If you wanted to locate information about referencing using the Harvard system, which would be the best search criteria?

a) Harvard OR Referencing
b) Harvard AND Referencing

Q18 What is a home page?

Q19 What is browsing history?

Q20 What are temporary internet files?

Q21 What are bookmarks?

Q22 What happens when you refresh a web page?

Q23 What is an advantage of tabbed browsing?

Q24 For this exercise you should match each term with its definition.

1. Metasearch engine	A. Website used for online discussions
2. Wiki	B. A way of checking a web page for updated content
3. Pop up blocker	C. A search engine that provides results from a number of search engines
4. Web feeds	D. A web page in which users collaborate to create the content
5. Forum	E. A way of preventing additional windows (often advertisements) when a web page loads

---

A SUMMARY OF KEY POINTS

In this chapter we have looked at the following key points.

> The need to be able to find, select and exchange electronic information, paying close attention to the quality of information located.

> The use of search tools and methods, with relevance to a range of electronic sources.

> The use of Boolean operators to conduct electronic searches where appropriate and evaluate the results of your searches with regards to validity, authority, currency and bias.

> The need to exchange information electronically and identification of key features and uses.

REFERENCES AND FURTHER READING REFERENCES AND FURTHER READING

Milner, A (2003) *Browsing the web (Essential computers).* London: DK Publishing

Websites

Interactive tutorial to improve internet skills: www.vts.intute.ac.uk/he/tutorial/social-research-methods

Extracts from the minimum core ICT framework

The central theme of this book has been the minimum core for ICT. To enable you to link to your own personal and professional development, extracts from the minimum core, Part B – Personal ICT Skills (pages 51– 55) are provided below:

PART B – PERSONAL ICT SKILLS

COMMUNICATION	Personal ICT skills for teaching and professional life
Communicate with others with/about ICT in an open and supportive manner	This requires trainee teachers to communicate with/about ICT in a manner that supports open discussion.
	Using discussion with/about ICT should include: • communicating with/about ICT concepts, skills and information with individuals and groups; • developing own and others' understanding of ICT concepts and skills; • promoting enquiry and sharing of ICT ideas; • promoting reflection as a community.
Assess own and other people's understanding	This requires trainee teachers to be able to assess their own and others' understanding.
	Assessment techniques should include: • personal review and reflection; • peer assessment; • questioning for understanding; • recognising and analysing misconceptions; • formal assessment methods such as written tests and observations.
Express yourself clearly and accurately	This requires trainee teachers to be able to: • communicate ICT concepts clearly and effectively; • use the language of ICT accurately.
	Appropriate communication should include: • structuring material; • use of debate around justification and fitness for purpose; • using illustrations, analogy and examples in purposeful contexts; • correct use of language such as ICT, software, functionality and systems; • appropriateness for audience and purpose.

COMMUNICATION	Personal ICT skills for teaching and professional life
Communicate with/about ICT in a variety of ways that suit and support the intended audience and recognise such use by others	This requires trainee teachers to be able to: • recognise differences in language needs; • formulate and provide appropriate responses; • recognise appropriate use of communication about/with ICT by others.
	Appropriate approaches should include: • checking how the information is received and explain terms or modify language appropriately; • adapting delivery according to level, needs and prior knowledge of the audience; • using pitch, pace, stress intonation and reinforce meaning using non-verbal cues; • interpreting non-verbal cues of others; • listening to the audience to identify the range of their ICT-related vocabulary; • identifying errors in terminology and correcting them.
Use appropriate techniques to reinforce oral communication, check how well the information is received and support the understanding of those listening	This requires trainee teachers to be able to use language and other forms of representation to: • reinforce oral communication of ICT concepts and skills; • check how well the information is received; • support the understanding of those listening.
	Trainee teachers should understand when a technique is being used to reinforce, check or support. Appropriate techniques should include: • provision of notes, summaries and examples; • modelling and demonstration; • repeating, rephrasing and summarising; • employing a range of questioning techniques; • requesting feedback and responding appropriately; • asking for a summary of information given; • the use of visual aids, including still and moving images and animations, equipment and artefacts.

PROCESSES	Personal ICT skills for teaching and professional life
Using ICT systems	This requires trainee teachers to: • select, interact and use ICT systems independently to meet a variety of needs in their personal and professional life; • evaluate the effectiveness of the ICT systems they have used; • manage information storage to enable efficient retrieval; • follow and understand the need for safety and security practices, particularly in relation to risks to children; • manage basic troubleshooting and know when to ask for support.
	Selection, interaction and use of ICT systems should be relevant to trainee teachers in their role and could include: • computers and computer-related hardware and software; • digital cameras, camcorders and other image capturing equipment; • interactive whiteboards; • digital television, video audio and other related multi-media equipment; • mobile phones and associated technology to support learning; • learning platforms; • graphic calculators.
	Using ICT systems should include the knowledge and skills to: • use correct procedures to start and shut down an ICT system; • use a communication device to access the internet; • select and use software applications to meet needs and solve problems; • select and use interface features and system facilities effectively to meet needs; • adjust system settings as appropriate to learner needs; • review the effectiveness of ICT tools to meet needs in order to inform future judgements; • manage files and folder structures to enable efficient information retrieval; • insert, remove, label and store media safely; • minimise physical stress when using ICT; • keep information secure; • understand the danger of computer viruses, and how to minimise risk; • understand the need to stay safe and to respect others when using ICT-based communication; • identify ICT problems and take appropriate action.

PROCESSES	Personal ICT skills for teaching and professional life
Finding, selecting and exchanging information	This requires trainee teachers to: • select and use a variety of sources of information independently to meet a variety of needs in their teaching and professional life; • access, search for, select and use ICT-based information and evaluate its fitness for purpose; • select and use ICT to communicate and exchange information for a variety of professional and personal purposes safely, responsibly and effectively; • evaluate their use of ICT-based communication and exchange of information.
	Finding, selecting and exchanging information should include the knowledge and skill to: • select and use appropriate sources of ICT-based and other forms of information which match requirements; • recognise copyright and other constraints on the use of information; • access, navigate and search internet sources of information purposefully and effectively; • use appropriate search techniques to locate information and design queries to select relevant information; • use discrimination in selecting information that matches requirements from a variety of sources and evaluate its fitness for purpose; • recognise characteristics of information, including intention and authority of provider, currency of information, reliability, accuracy, relevance, potential bias, confidentiality, ownership, applicability to general or specific contexts; • create, access, read and respond appropriately to e-mail and other ICT-based communication and adapt style and content to suit audience; • manage efficient storage of ICT-based communications, attachments and contact details.

PROCESSES	Personal ICT skills for teaching and professional life
Developing and presenting information	This requires trainee teachers to: • enter, develop and format information independently to suit its meaning and purpose and to meet a variety of needs in their teaching and professional life, including texts and tables, images, numbers and records; • bring together information to suit audience content and purpose; • present information in ways that are fit for purpose and audience; • evaluate the selection and use of ICT tools and facilities used to present information.
	Developing and presenting information should include the knowledge and skill to: • enter, organise, develop, refine and format information, applying editing techniques to meet needs; • use appropriate page layout; • enter and format text to maximise clarity and enhance presentation; • create and format tables to maximise clarity of the structure and content of information and to enhance presentation; • obtain, insert, size, crop and position images that are fit for purpose; • enter, develop and organise numerical information in ways that are fit for purpose, including the use of formulas and functions; • format numerical information appropriately; • create and develop charts and graphs to suit the numerical information using suitable labels; • enter, organise, select and edit records using field names and headings, data types and unique record identifiers where appropriate; • sort records on one or more fields in ascending or descending order; • bring together and organise components of images and text • organise information of different forms or from different sources to achieve a purpose; • work accurately and proofread, using software facilities where appropriate • produce information that is fit for purpose and audience using accepted layouts and conventions as appropriate; • evaluate the effectiveness of ICT tools to meet presentation needs; • review and modify work as it progresses to ensure the result is fit for purpose and audience, and to inform future judgements.

Answers to key questions

3. Communicating ICT

Q1   c) Physical components of the computer

Q2   a) Programs used by the computer

Q3   b) Mouse, c) Keyboard, d) Speakers

Q4   c) An operating system

Q5   b) CPU

Q6   a) Temporary memory

Q7   c) A mix of skill levels

Q8   d) Yes, but don't make an issue, and be supportive

Q9   b) A laptop

Q10 b) Learners learn more effectively by identifying own areas for development, d) It encourages reflection

Q11 1. Internet – E. Global network of computers;
2. World wide web – A. Interconnected pages accessed via the internet;
3. URL – F. Address of a web page;
4. Internet Explorer – C. Web browser;
5. Windows Explorer – D. Windows file management system;
6. Search engine – B. Used to search for information over the web

Q12 a) The font size seems fine. The handout comprises all text. Adding images to support the instructions would assist. They could be used to show buttons to click and at various stages examples of what they should be seeing.
b) The presentation could be revised to show bullet points, rather than large amounts of text, allowing the text size to be enlarged. Images could be used selectively to demonstrate key points. The bulk of the text could be provided to learners in the form of a supporting handout. Questions could be used to check understanding throughout the session.
c) The handout is useful to support the session, however, the use of a projector displaying a presentation which contains the main points would be more effective for a large group. Questions and a range of activities could be used to check understanding throughout the session.
d) This is a case where images, even drawings on a whiteboard, could be used to enhance the session considerably. The language used should be at the appropriate level for the learners.

Q13 a) Formative assessment only takes place at the end of the session: **False**
b) Initial assessment is the same as diagnostic assessment: **False**
c) Question and answer is one method of formative assessment: **True**
d) Summative assessment takes place at the end of a course: **True**
e) Peer assessment is undertaken the teacher: **False**
f) Self assessment is mainly ineffective: **False**
g) Diagnostic assessment often takes place at the end of the course: **False**
h) Assessment for learning always takes place at the start of the course: **False**
i) Examination is one method of summative assessment: **True**
j) Diagnostic assessment is more detailed than initial assessment: **True**

Q14 a) Observation can be an effective way of assessing practical skills, however, it may not assess understanding or cognitive skills. If done discretely and informally, observation can help to reduce learner anxiety. Because the task is to be workbook based, you need to ensure that no learners are disadvantaged, for example, learners with dyslexia or visual impairment.
b) Whilst an interview is an excellent way of getting to know learners on a one-to-one basis, it may not present evidence of practical skills, unless supported with evidence of prior learning. You should avoid relying on learners' own self assessment at an early stage in the course. Some learners may overstate and some may understate their skills, giving an unreliable result. It may be more effective to combine the interview with a practical task.
c) A homework task has the advantage that learners can work on the task at their own pace, allowing differentiation. Authenticity may be an issue though and you cannot be certain that the work is that of the learner or whether they have had any assistance in completing the task.

Q15 a) This instruction makes the assumption that the learners know the procedure for logging on to the computers. They may not have used a keyboard or mouse before and therefore may not know how to enter the user name and password. Revised instructions may also include how to operate the mouse and keyboard.
b) This instruction makes a number of assumptions. The learners may not have used a word processor before and a font size may mean nothing to them. Revised instructions could include an explanation of font size and guiding the learners step by step, supported by questions to encourage learners to find answers for themselves.
c) This instruction falls short in a number of ways. Firstly the learners may not know how to access the calculator application. Once opened, the learners may need instruction regarding the use of the calculator. Revised instructions could include guiding the learners through the steps to open the application and how to use the calculator using keyboard or mouse.
d) You need to be very careful about giving an instruction of this type. New computer users may instinctively reach for the on/off button. Once more there is a need to give step-by-step instructions and explain why the computer should not be shut down using the on/off button.
e) With this instruction it is assumed that learners know what Microsoft Word, a shortcut, and the desktop are. Learners could be encouraged to contribute what they know by the effective use of questions and guided step by step through the process of opening a shortcut.

In all of the above examples it is important the terminology be introduced and explained in conjunction with the instructions.

4. Personal, social and cultural factors influencing ICT learning and development

Q1   b) Unsolicited e-mail

Q2   c) An attempt to obtain passwords and account details via fraudulent e-mail.

Q3   d) A computer program designed with malicious intent

Q4   c) The gap between those who have access to digital technology and those who do not

Q5   a) To protect a computer from external attacks

Q6   d) None of the above

Q7   b) Not opening attachments from unknown sources

Q8   b) Special Educational Needs and Disability Act

Q9   b) Illegal copying of software, c) Illegal file sharing

Q10   a) Hacking into computers, d) Distribution of viruses

Q11   a) Broadband is available throughout the entire United Kingdom: **False**
b) Search engine results are not screened for unsuitable links: **True**
c) Organisational policies regarding ICT do not apply to learners: **False**
d) ICT legislation does not apply within educational organisations: **False**
e) A virus can only be activated by opening an e-mail: **False**
f) Phishing e-mails look very different to genuine e-mails: **False**
g) Organisational settings may not prevent access to unsuitable websites: **True**
h) When you purchase a music CD you own the copyright: **False**
i) Broadband is not the only way to access the internet: **True**
j) Under 18s cannot be prosecuted for illegal copying: **False**

Q12   a) Speak to learners to assure them that they will get all the support they need in class. Make them aware of ICT facilities available within the organisation.
b) These facilities may include a learning resource centre, short courses, library resources and books to support development of their ICT skills.
c) Ensure that you use language that is relevant to all learners. When using computers you could give an activity for learners to work through at their own pace. This will allow you to spend time with any learners who need additional support. You could also encourage group work and mix the four learners with more confident members of the group, thus encouraging peer teaching.

Q13   a) Low confidence may be an issue within this group. They may not have access to computers at home. The learners may have other children who do not yet attend school, so childcare may need to be offered. They may also have spiky profiles in the area of literacy, numeracy and language, so may need support at different levels for different elements of the course.
b) The use of the calculator option on the computer could form an initial introduction to computer use. Following this, spreadsheets are an excellent way of combining maths and ICT skills and could be used to create a weekly or monthly family budget.
c) A word processor could be used to get learners to create documents which may include CVs, birthday invitations and job applications, depending on learner requirement.

d) Video cameras could be used to record learners' mock interviews. Video conferencing could allow the learners to talk to one another and develop communication skills. Learners could be encouraged to create slideshows and present to the group.

Q14 a) Disability Discrimination Act (SENDA)

b) The learner may have problems using a keyboard and not be able to type very fast. They may also have difficulties using a mouse.

c) A range of keyboards and mice are available to suit a range of learners. It is important to speak to the learner to find out what they require, rather than making assumptions. Sticky keys is an option provided with Windows that assists when learners can only press one key at a time. (Press shift 5 times to experiment with this.)

Q15 a) A primary school teacher needs a wide range of ICT skills. They need to be able to use generic and office software in order to be able to support pupils and also need to use e-mail and internet. They will be required to keep student records and for this purpose will probably use spreadsheet or database software. Primary schools now include interactive whiteboards and therefore the teacher will also need to be able to use these and also perform basic troubleshooting within the classroom.

b) A solicitor will need to use office software. They will also need to communicate with other professionals, clients and colleagues electronically. They may also use video conferencing software.

c) A nurse will need to maintain patient records and therefore will need to be able to use software created for this purpose, which may be specific to the organisation or generic office software. They will need accurate keyboard skills. They may also be required to use generic diagnostic software.

d) Journalists will require good word processing skills and be able to type with both speed and accuracy. They will need to use e-mail including attachments and also need to access the web for research.

Q16 **Malware** is the general term used to refer to software created with malicious intent.
A **trojan** is software that appears innocent, for example a game or computer utility, but ultimately is created with malicious intent.
Spyware is software that can be inadvertently installed on a computer and monitors the user's actions.
Cookies enable user's details to be recalled when revisiting a website. They may be disabled within some **web browsers.**

5. ICT tools

Q1 c) Create letters and reports

Q2 c) An instruction to perform a calculation

Q3 d) An essential part of a function

Q4 b) Transition

Q5 a) Images, b) Text, c) Sound clips, d) Movie clips

Q6 a) Records

Q7 b) Is a unique identifier

Q8   a) Decrease the size of the margins, c) Reduce the font size

Q9   c) =A1+A9

Q10 c) Automatically and manually

Q11 1. xlS B. Spreadsheet
      2. .doc C. Word processor
      3. pps A. Presentation
      4. .mdb D. Database

Q12 1. Used for typing a letter B.12
      2. Used for slideshow heading A.32
      3. Used for slideshow text D.26
      4. Used for a header or footer C.8

Q13 a) database, b) may, c) need not, d) should not, e) do, f) is

Q14 a) (i) =C2-B2; b) (ii) Bold, Left aligned; c) (i) =AVERAGE(D2:D6); d) (iii) =MAX(D2:D6)

Q15 a) (i) Text; b) (ii) Number, integer; c) (ii) Student Number; d) (i) >=45; e) (iii) >02/11/09

Q16 a) autoshapes; b) bold and centred; c) tabs; d) left aligned; e) italics

Q17 a) (ii) Slide 1 and slide 3; b) (iii) Slide sorter view; c) (ii) Slide 2; (d) (i) To display a website

Q18 a) Use the page setup option to change the page to be one page wide by one page tall.
      b) By changing the slides per page to three in the handouts section of the print dialog box. This will give space on the right for the learners to write notes.
      c) Printing in greyscale would be the option to use. This is accessed via the print dialog box.
      d) The collate option should be selected by ticking the collate box which is accessed via the print dialog box.
      e) Before printing any document it is always wise to use the print preview option which is accessed via the toolbar or menus.

6. Purposeful use of ICT

Q1   c) Using ICT in combination with a traditional teaching approach

Q2   a) Electronic learning

Q3   a) Virtual Learning Environment

Q4   b) Discussion facilities, c) Hyperlinks to websites, d) On-line tests

Q5   b) No internet access

Q6   b) Combination of different media

Q7   a) Appealing to a range of learning styles

Q8   b) Some areas may not have resources available, c) Unknown quality of resources

Q9 c) Free Skype to Skype video calls

Q10 d) Consider the appropriateness of ICT and how it can enhance learning

Q11 You have a couple of options here. This depends on whether the learners have access to e-mail or mobile phone, or a combination of the two. You could send an e-mail or text message to the group and ask them to reply to confirm that they have read your message and feedback on progress.

Q12 You could recreate the exercise using word processing software. Text boxes could be used instead of cards and learners could use an interactive whiteboard to drag the boxes to the appropriate place. This could also be done without a whiteboard, using a mouse to drag the boxes.

Q13 You could ask a question and get the learners to work in groups and text you back the answer to the question. This could be a fun way to end the session and help check learning is taking place at the same time.

Q14 The internet connection could be used to allow the learners to search for design and embroidery examples. They could also research historical embroidery and locate information regarding stitches.

Q15 a) Mobile broadband cannot be used with a laptop computer: **False**
b) Personal computers are the most effective way of using ICT in teaching: **False**
c) ICT is inappropriate for use in community settings: **False**
d) ICT can be used to enhance teaching and motivate learners: **True**
e) Blended learning involves the use of ICT: **True**
f) Poorly used ICT can demotivate learners: **True**
g) A VLE can be accessed remotely: **True**
h) Skype requires an internet connection: **True**
i) Multimedia is mainly relevant to visual learners: **False**
j) Text written on an interactive whiteboard can be saved: **True**

Q16 **Mobile** broadband can be used when an **internet** connection is not available and is particularly relevant for use in **community** settings.
Mobile phones can have many different uses in the **classroom**. The **bluetooth** and **text** facilities can be used to send messages between the group and to/from the teacher.
Resource banks are depositories of **resources** created by others and can save **time** compared to creating your own. However, they should be **evaluated** prior to use.

Q17 a) Learners can use a range of facilities on a mobile phone. They can text answers to questions, photograph notes written on the board, use calculator facilities and video demonstrations.
b) A range of software is available on personal computers that can be used to enhance learning. This could include creation of computer-based quizzes, activities and educational games. Learners could conduct internet research under tutor supervision.
c) Digital cameras can be used to photograph notes written on the board. The video facilities can be used to record presentation or demonstrations. Learners' work can be photographed to create displays or portfolio evidence.
d) Video cameras can be used to record presentations or demonstrations. They could be used on field trips to replay elements of the visit and encourage further discussion.
e) Video conferencing can be used to allow remote groups to interact. Learners at another location or organisation could work collaboratively and benefit from wider knowledge.

Q18 a) By nominating just one member of the group they are in danger of excluding the rest. The lecturer should ensure that at some stage all of the learners are able to use this resource and be clear at the outset that all will be involved. They may ask for volunteers initially and if one member of the group is more knowledgeable in camera use they could use the opportunity to encourage peer teaching.

b) For this example the lecturer needs to be sure that the learners are well directed. They should supervise the activity and ensure that all learners know how to use the available resources.

c) The lecturer should not assume that all learners have access to a mobile phone. They should give other options. For example, e-mail. They may pair learners and ensure that one of the pair has access to a mobile phone and is happy to use the phone for this purpose.

d) Asking the group to sort themselves is rarely a good idea. Some learners may feel excluded. If the lecturer sorts the groups to ensure that one member of the group has strong ICT skills they could encourage peer teaching, ensuring that this learner does not dominate with the task.

e) The use of the remote mouse merely makes it easier for the lecturer to advance slides, it does not enhance learning. The mouse and keyboard could be passed around the group encouraging their input. They could be asked to type text into the presentation, further involving them in the session.

7. ICT systems

Q1 b) Change the resolution to 800 x 600

Q2 c) A location on a disk or computer that can contain other folders and files

Q3 a) The folder is expanded to show sub folders

Q4 d) 1GB

Q5 b) CD-R/RW

Q6 a) CTRL-ALT-DELETE

Q7 c) It remains in its original location

Q8 d) Digital Versatile Disk

Q9 a) Yes. A DVD can only be read in a DVD drive

Q10 a) DVD-RW, c) CD-RW

Q11 **CDs** generally have a storage capacity of 700MB. The reusable version is known as **CD-RW**, whereas the non-reusable version is know as **CD-R**.
DVDs generally have a storage capacity of 4.7GB. The reusable version is known as **DVD-RW,** whereas the non-reusable version is know as **DVD-R**.
Floppy disks can be corrupted by being placed near a mobile phone.

Q12 a) The left side of Windows Explorer displays files: **False**
b) The control panel can be launched by pressing CTRL-ALT-DELETE: **False**
c) Clicking on the size heading in Windows Explorer will reduce the file size: **False**
d) Using Windows explorer is not the only way to create folders: **True**

e) Left clicking and dragging a file to the required location is one way to copy a file: **False**

f) Deleting a folder will not delete the contents: **False**

g) Desktop settings can be revised via the control panel display option: **True**

h) Folders are used to organise files in Windows Explorer: **True**

i) Windows Explorer can be accessed via the control panel: **False**

j) Restarting the computer will solve any software problems: **False**

Q13 a) To store teaching resources to be accessed at home and work: **USB memory**

b) To save documents and transfer from an older laptop for backup purposes: **Floppy disk**

c) To save a large quantity of videos and images for use in the classroom: **DVD**

d) To back up your important documents on a weekly basis: **CD-RW**

Q14 The answers below give first steps suggestions for basic troubleshooting.

a) It is worth checking your keyboard connection if you are tying to type but nothing appears on screen.

b) Check your printer connection and that the printer is switched on. You should also check that there is paper in the printer and you do not have a paper jam.

c) Try pressing CTRL-ALT DELETE to activate the task manager and close down the non-responding program.

d) If a program isn't responding as you expect you should close down the program and restart the computer to see if this resolves the problem.

e) This could be a simple power problem. Check that the computer is plugged in and switched on at the mains and also that the power cable is securely attached.

Q15 1. Defragment C. Rearranging files on the hard disk to improve performance
2. Scan/check disk E. Searches for errors on a hard disk
3. System Restore B. Used to rollback system settings to a previous point in time
4. Backup A. Saves copies of files to use if problems occur with originals
5. Disk Clean up D. Searches for unwanted files to create space on the hard disk

Q16 a) E

b) The folder is expanded to view the sub folders.

c) The above process is reversed, hiding the sub folders.

d) ICT, Language, Literacy and Numeracy

e) 2

f) By right clicking on the disk and selecting Properties. The used and available space are visible on the general tab.

g) The quickest way to do this would be to format the disk. Right click on the disk and select format to access this dialog box.

8 Finding, selecting and exchanging information

Q1 a) You must use Boolean operators when searching websites: **False**

b) Web directories are more effective than search engines for browsing topics on the web: **True**

c) Web directories are good for accessing local information: **True**

d) Search engines must be used to access a web page: **False**

e) The web pages at the top of the search results list will be the most relevant: **True**

f) Every search engine gives the same results: **False**

g) Websites are always a reliable source of information: **False**

h) When evaluating a website, the main consideration is how the text is presented: **False**

i) Sending an e-mail does not require internet access: **False**

k) An e-mail can be sent to a number of people at the same time: **True**

Q2 a) Anyone can publish information on the world wide web, c) Each website should be considered on its own merits and evaluated accordingly

Q3 d) Unlimited

Q4 b) Government websites

Q5 c) Must cite the source to acknowledge the author's intellectual copyright and ask permission prior to use

Q6 b) e-books are digital versions of traditional books

Q7 b) Forward

Q8 c) Distribution list

Q9 a) Joe.bloggs.bt, c) John.smith

Q10 a) Inbox

Q11 d) Outbox

Q12 a) The use of Boolean operators can enhance and support electronic searches, however, they **may** not be supported by **all** search engines.
b) There are **many** search engines which can produce a range of different search results.
c) **OR** can be used to increase the number of hits when searching electronically, whereas **NOT** and **AND** are used to reduce the number of hits.
d) Complete phrases can be searched for via the use of **speech marks** (" "), however, they can have limited use unless used carefully and may results in too few hits.
e) When a list of results is presented following a search, it is important to be aware of the sponsored links which have been **paid** for by an advertiser.

Q13 b) Pages containing the phrase 'Curriculum Design Stenhouse".

Q14 b) humanis*

Q15 b) literature AND review

Q16 b) psychoanalysis NOT Freud

Q17 b) Harvard AND Referencing

Q18 This is the page that is viewed when the web browser is launched. It can also be accessed via the home button on the browser toolbar.

Q19 Browsing history is a list of web pages that a user has visited.

Q20 Temporary internet files are copies of web pages that are stored on your computer.

Q21 Bookmarks are links to websites and can be accessed quickly via your browser.

Q22 The web page is reloaded. This is useful if the page does not load at the first attempt.

Q23 With tabbed browsing several web pages can be viewed at the same time.

Q24
1. Metasearch engine C. A search engine that provides results from a number of search engines
2. Wiki D. A web page in which users collaborate to create the content
3. Pop up blocker E. A way of preventing additional windows (often advertisements) when a web page loads
4. Web Feeds B. A way of checking a web page for updated content
5. Forum A. Website used for online discussions